ELECTRIC BASS BOOK 3

ESSENTIAL TECHNIQUE for Band

INTERMEDIATE TO ADVANCED STUDIES

TIM LAUTZENHEISER • JOHN HIGGINS • CHARLES MENGHINI
PAUL LAVENDER • TOM C. RHODES • DON BIERSCHENK

To create an account, visit:
www.essentialelementsinteractive.com

Student Activation Code
E3EB-0637-3664-5744

ISBN 979-835013705-7

B♭ MAJOR

1. SCALE AND ARPEGGIO

2. EXERCISE IN THIRDS

3. ARPEGGIO STUDY

4. TWO-PART ETUDE

5. CHROMATIC SCALE

6. BALANCE BUILDER

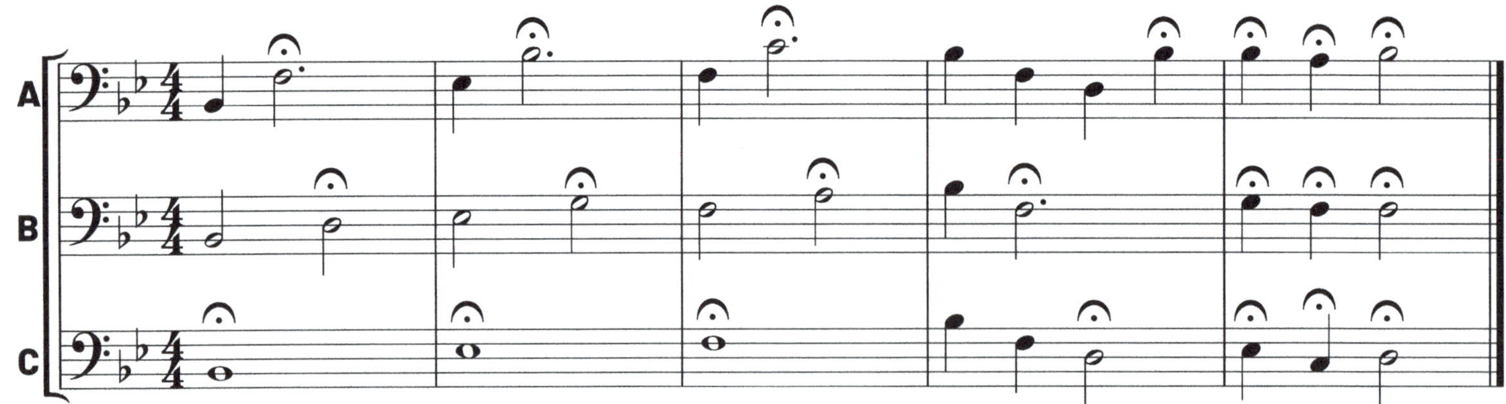

THEORY

divisi or *div.*	Divide the written parts among players, usually into two parts, with equal numbers playing each part.
unison or *a2*	All players play the same part (usually found after a *divisi* section).

7. CHORALE

8. GREAT GATE OF KIEV

Modeste Mussorgsky

9. CHILDREN'S SHOES

African American Spiritual

English composer **George Frideric Handel** (1685–1759) is among the best known composers of the **Baroque Period (1600–1750)**. *Sound an Alarm* (from *Judas Maccabaeus*) and his most famous work, the *Hallelujah Chorus* (from *Messiah*), are two well-known melodies from his **oratorios** – large scale works for solo voices, chorus, and orchestra.

HISTORY

10. SOUND AN ALARM

George Frideric Handel

11. HALLELUJAH CHORUS

George Frideric Handel

12. RHYTHM RAP *Clap the rhythm while counting and tapping.*

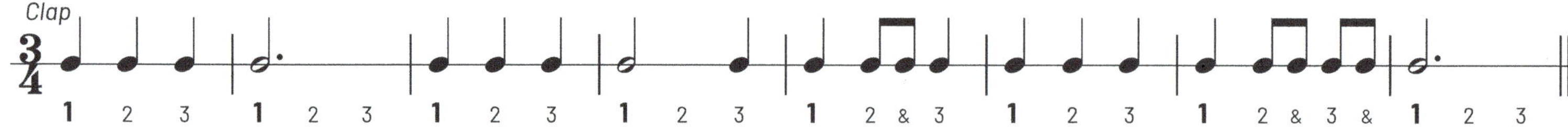

THEORY

3/8 Time Signature

3 = **3 beats** per measure
8 = **Eighth** note gets one beat

♪ = 1 beat ♩ = 2 beats ♩. = 3 beats

3/8 time is usually played with a slight emphasis on the 1st beat of each measure. In faster music, this primary beat will make the music feel like it's counted "in 1."

13. RHYTHM RAP *Compare this exercise with No. 12.*

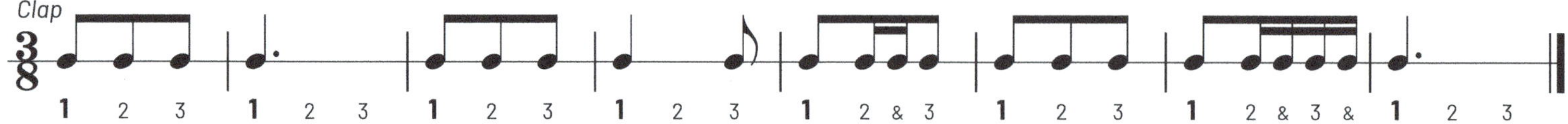

14. WALTZ PETITE

15. MOLLY BANN

English Folksong

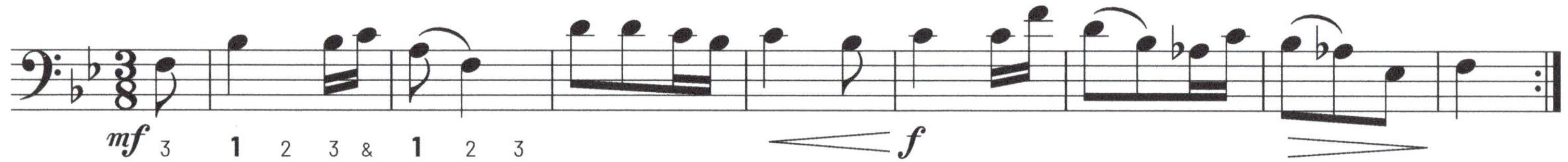

THEORY

9/8 Time Signature

9 = **9 beats** per measure
8 = **Eighth** note gets one beat

♪ = 1 beat ♩. = 3 beats
♩ = 2 beats 𝅗𝅥. = 6 beats

9/8 time is usually played with a slight emphasis on the **1st**, **4th**, and **7th** beats of each measure. This divides the measure into 3 groups of 3 beats each. In faster music, these three primary beats will make the music feel like it's counted "in 3."

16. RHYTHM RAP *Clap the rhythm while counting and tapping.*

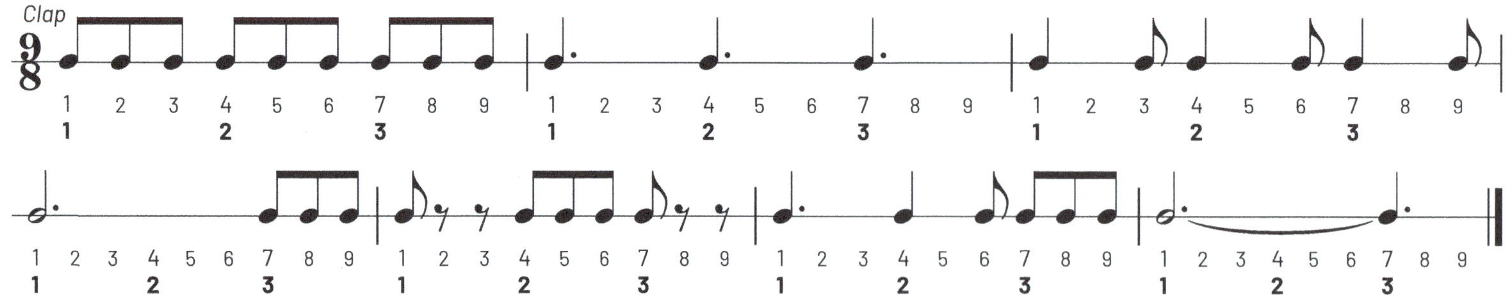

17. SUNDAY AT NINE

G MINOR

THEORY

Minor Keys

Minor keys and their scales sound different from major keys because of their different pattern of whole and half steps. Each minor key is *relative* or "related" to the major key with the same key signature.

The simplest form of a minor key is called **natural minor**. Two other types are **harmonic minor** and **melodic minor**, each of which have certain altered tones.

18. NATURAL MINOR *Practice both upper and lower octaves*

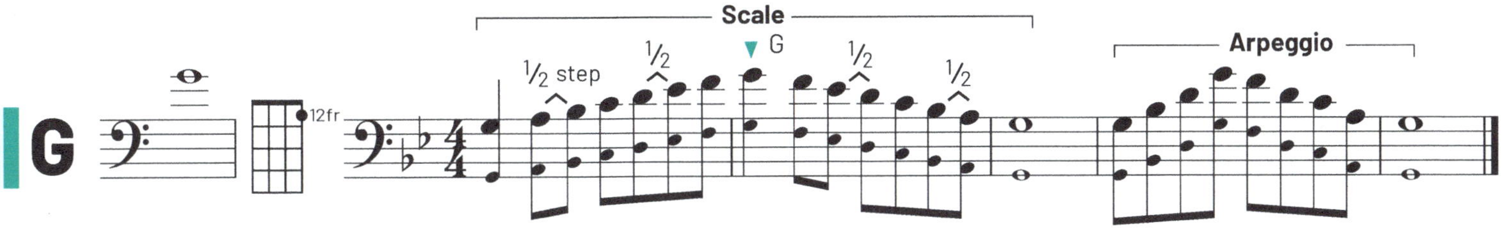

Scale — ½ step — ½ — G — ½ — ½ — Arpeggio

G — 12fr

19. HARMONIC MINOR

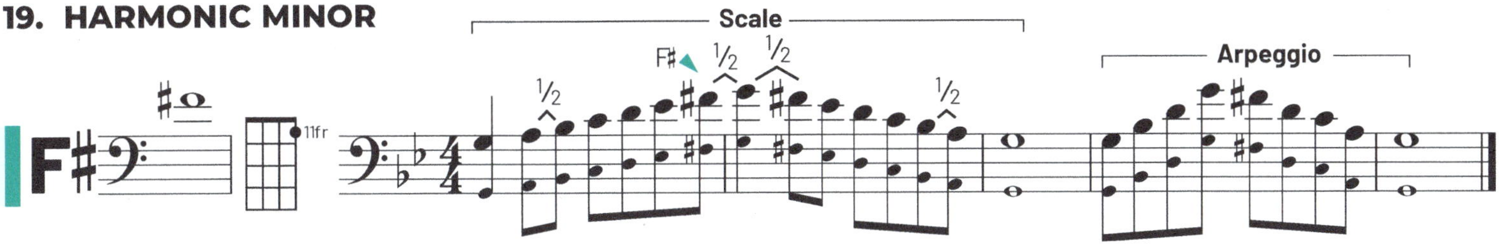

Scale — ½ — F♯ — ½ — ½ — ½ — Arpeggio

F♯ — 11fr

20. PAT-A-PAN — French

Moderato *mf*

21. THE SLEDGEHAMMER SONG — Russian

Moderato *f* *mp* *f*

22. ESSENTIAL ELEMENTS QUIZ – AUSTRALIAN FOLK SONG — Australian

E♭ MAJOR

23. SCALE AND ARPEGGIO

24. EXERCISE IN THIRDS

25. ARPEGGIO STUDY

26. TWO-PART ETUDE

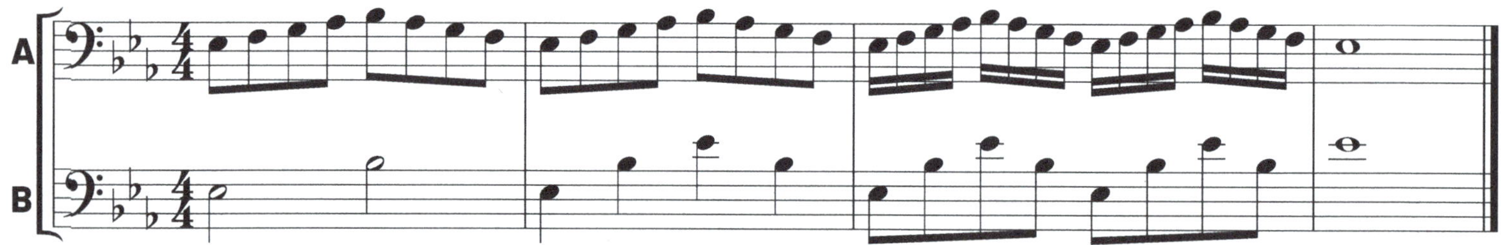

27. CHROMATIC SCALE

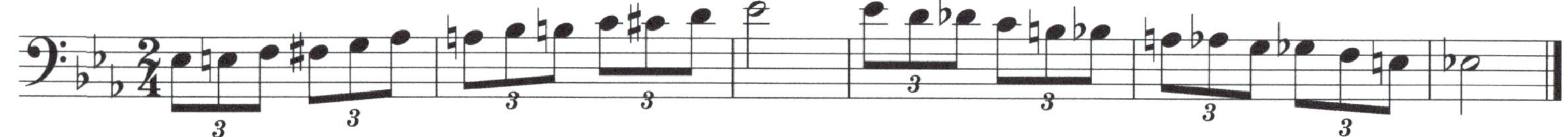

28. BALANCE BUILDER

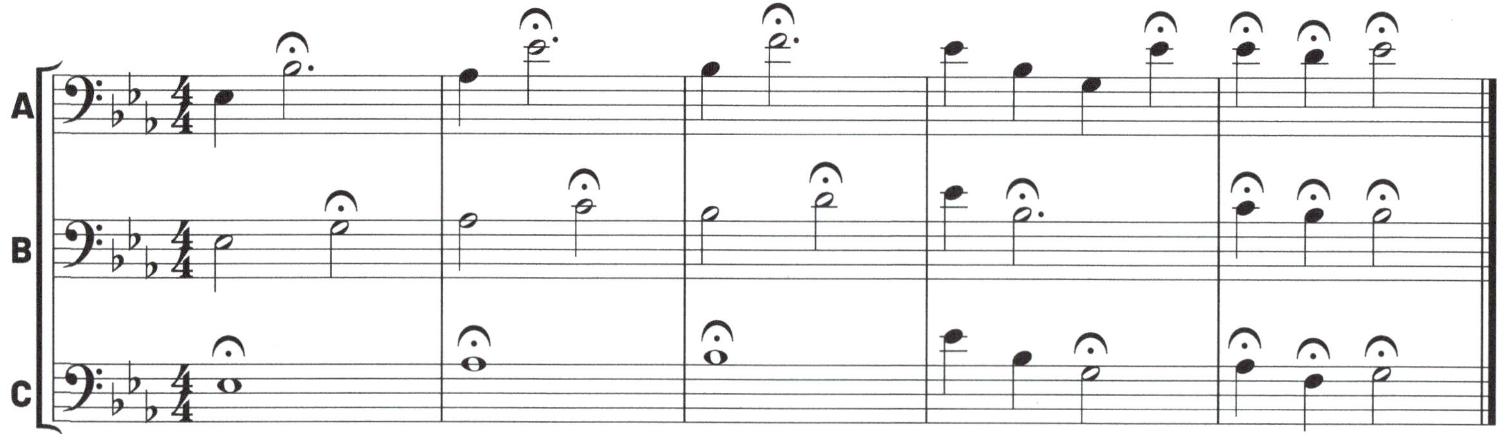

29. CHORALE

Austrian composer **Johann Strauss Jr.** (1825–1899) is also known as "The Waltz King." He wrote some of the world's most famous waltzes (dances in 3/4 meter). This waltz is from *Die Fledermaus* ("The Bat"), Strauss' most famous **operetta**. Operettas were the forerunners of today's musicals, such as *Oklahoma*, *The Sound of Music*, *The Phantom of the Opera*, *Wicked*, and *Hamilton*.

35. JACK'S THE MAN

THEORY

12/8 Time Signature

= **12 beats** per measure
= **Eighth note** gets one beat

♪ = 1 beat ♩. = 3 beats 𝅗𝅥.‿♩. = 9 beats
♩ = 2 beats 𝅗𝅥. = 6 beats 𝅝. = 12 beats

12/8 time is usually played with a slight emphasis on the **1st**, **4th**, **7th,** and **10th** beats of each measure. This divides the measure into 4 groups of 3 beats each. These four primary beats will make the music feel like it's counted "in 4."

36. RHYTHM RAP *Clap the rhythm while counting and tapping.*

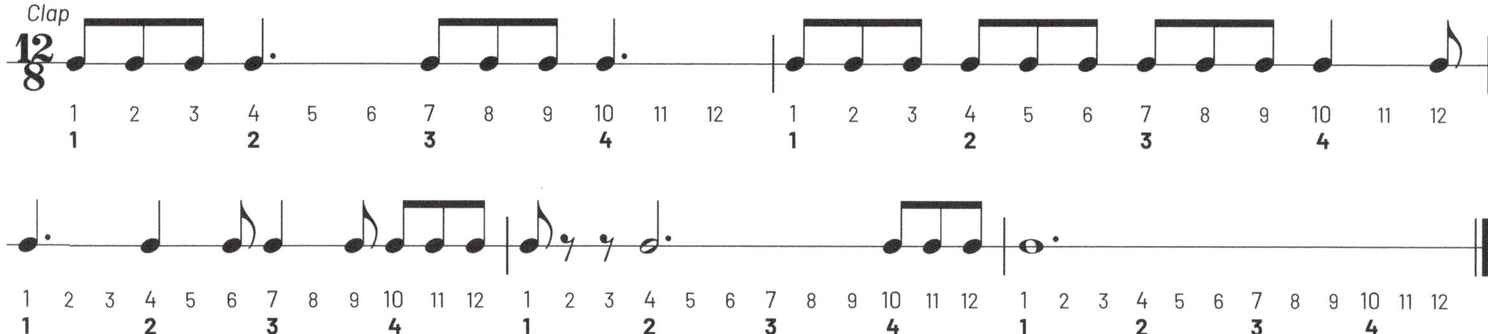

37. SERENADE

38. WITH THINE EYES

C MINOR

39. NATURAL MINOR

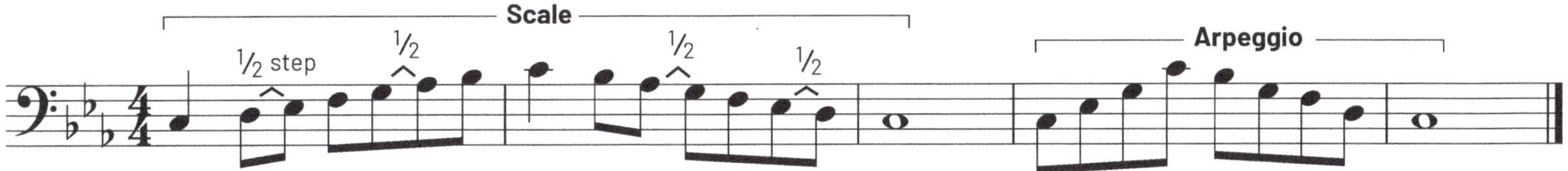

40. HARMONIC MINOR

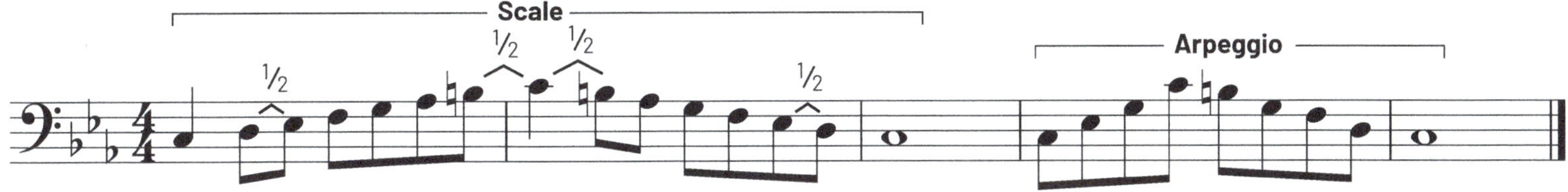

HISTORY

Even today, **Native American Indian music** continues to be an important part of tribal dancing ceremonies, using Apache fiddles, rattles, flutes, and log drums to accompany simple songs. American composer **Charles Wakefield Cadman** (1881–1946) wrote this song in 1914 based on Indian melodies he researched throughout his lifetime.

41. SONG OF THE WEEPING SPIRIT

Native American Indian Melody
Adapt. Charles Wakefield Cadman

42. SCOTTISH LEGEND

Amy Marcy Beach

43. ESSENTIAL ELEMENTS QUIZ *Which measures sound major and which ones minor?*

F MAJOR

44. SCALE AND ARPEGGIO *Practice both upper and lower octaves.*

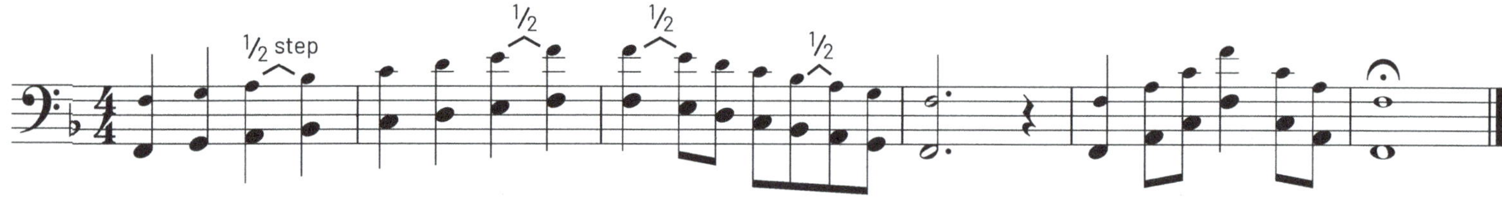

45. EXERCISE IN THIRDS

46. ARPEGGIO STUDY

47. TWO-PART ETUDE

48. CHROMATIC SCALE

49. BALANCE BUILDER

50. CHORALE

51. REST ALERT

52. RHYTHM RAP

53. ISLAND SONG

French composer **Claude Debussy** (1862–1918) created moods and "impressions" with his music. While earlier composers used music to describe events (such as Tchaikovsky's *1812 Overture*), Debussy's new ideas helped shape today's music. The style of art and music created in this time is called "impressionism." The first automobile was produced during Debussy's lifetime. He died the same year that World War I ended.

HISTORY

54. THE LITTLE CHILD

Claude Debussy

Triplets with Rests

Triplets that start or end with a rest are usually marked with a bracket ⌐3¬

THEORY

55. TRIPLET AND REST VARIATIONS

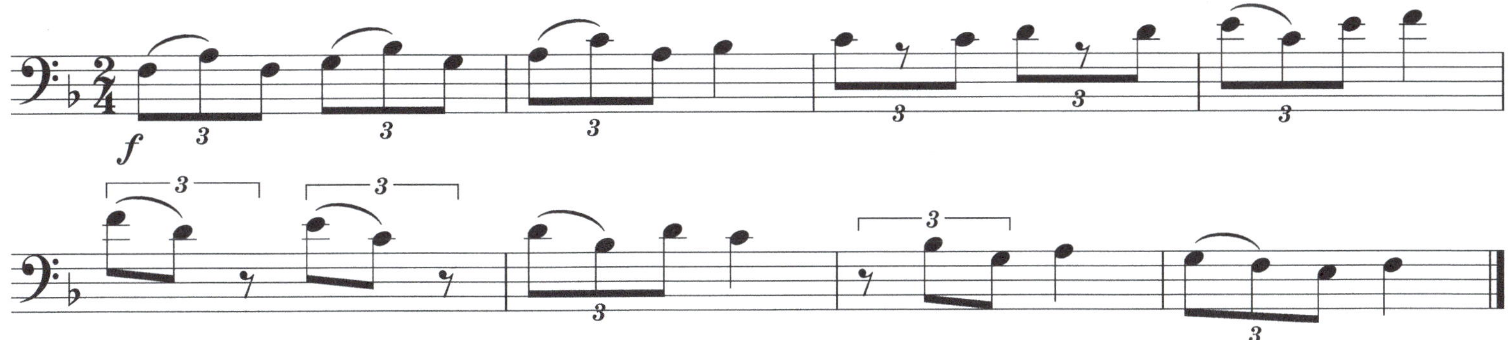

56. TURKEY IN THE STRAW

American Folk Song

57. ESSENTIAL ELEMENTS QUIZ

Write the first 2 lines of exercise 56 in cut time.

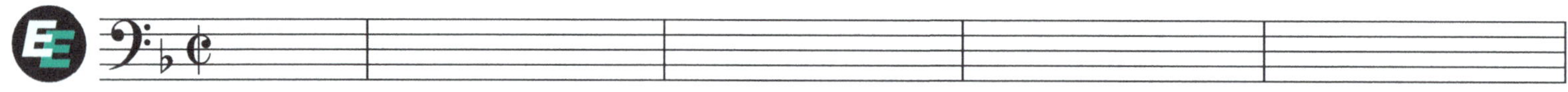

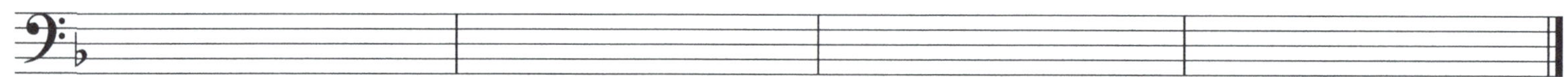

THEORY

Sixteenth Notes and Rests in 6/8, 3/8, 9/8, 12/8

♬ = 1/2 beat 𝄿 = 1/2 beat ♩ = 2 beats 𝄽 = 2 beats
♪ = 1 beat 𝄾 = 1 beat ♩. = 3 beats 𝄽. = 3 beats

58. RHYTHM RAP

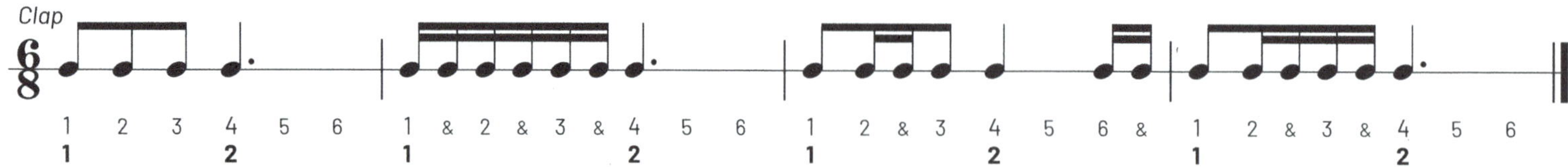

59. SONATINA

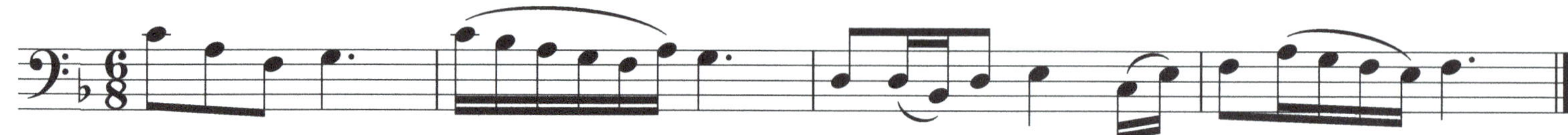

D MINOR

60. NATURAL MINOR

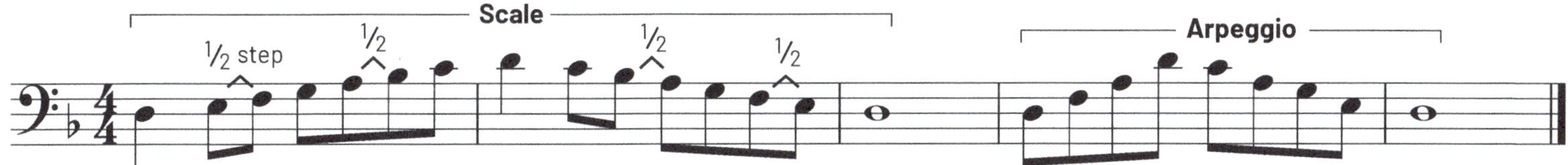

61. HARMONIC MINOR

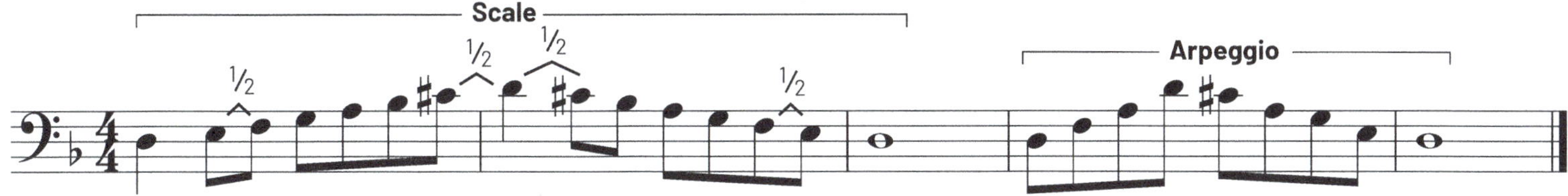

62. COSSACK MARCH

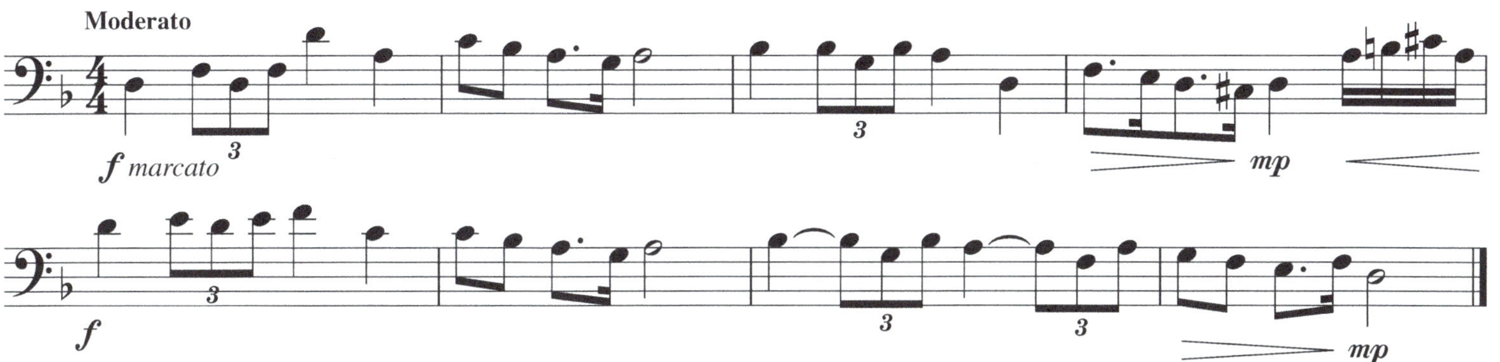

63. SLAVONIC DANCE NO. 2

Antonin Dvorák

64. ESSENTIAL ELEMENTS QUIZ – THE PRETTY GIRL

Irish

A♭ MAJOR

65. SCALE AND ARPEGGIO *Practice both upper and lower octaves.*

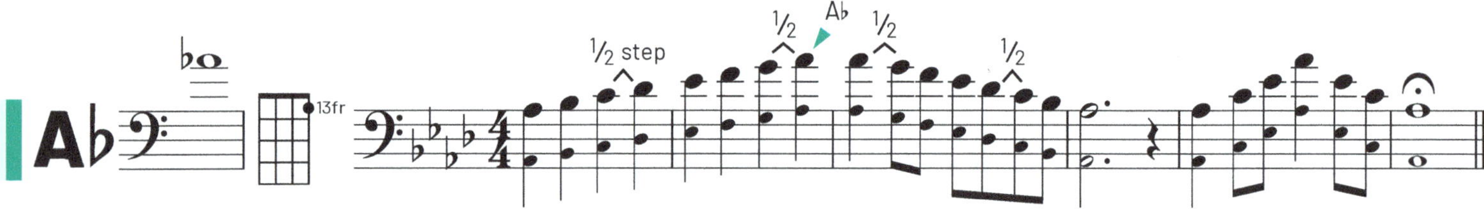

66. EXERCISE IN THIRDS

67. ARPEGGIO STUDY

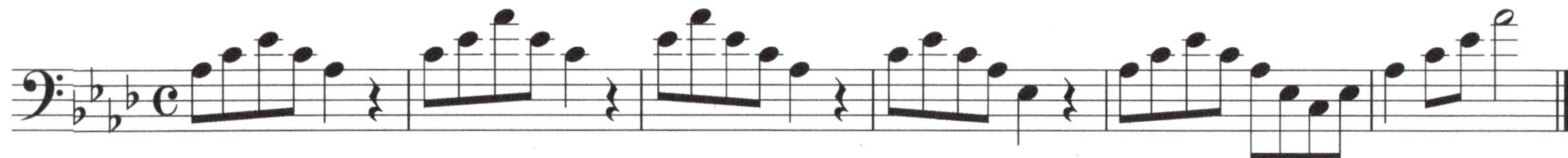

68. TWO-PART ETUDE *Practice both upper and lower octaves.*

69. CHROMATIC SCALE

70. BALANCE BUILDER

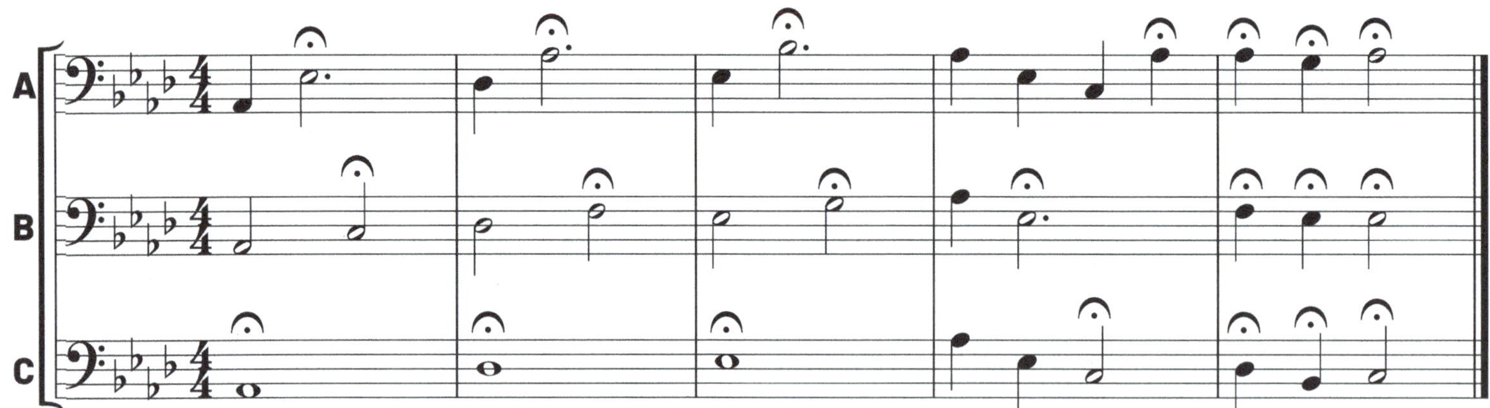

71. CHORALE

HISTORY

The Star Spangled Banner is the national anthem of the United States of America. Francis Scott Key wrote the words during the 1814 battle at Fort McHenry. He listened to the sounds of the fighting throughout the night while being detained on a ship. At dawn, he saw the American flag still flying over the fort. He was inspired to write these words, which were later set to the melody of a popular English song.

72. THE STAR SPANGLED BANNER

Words by Francis Scott Key
Music by John Stafford Smith

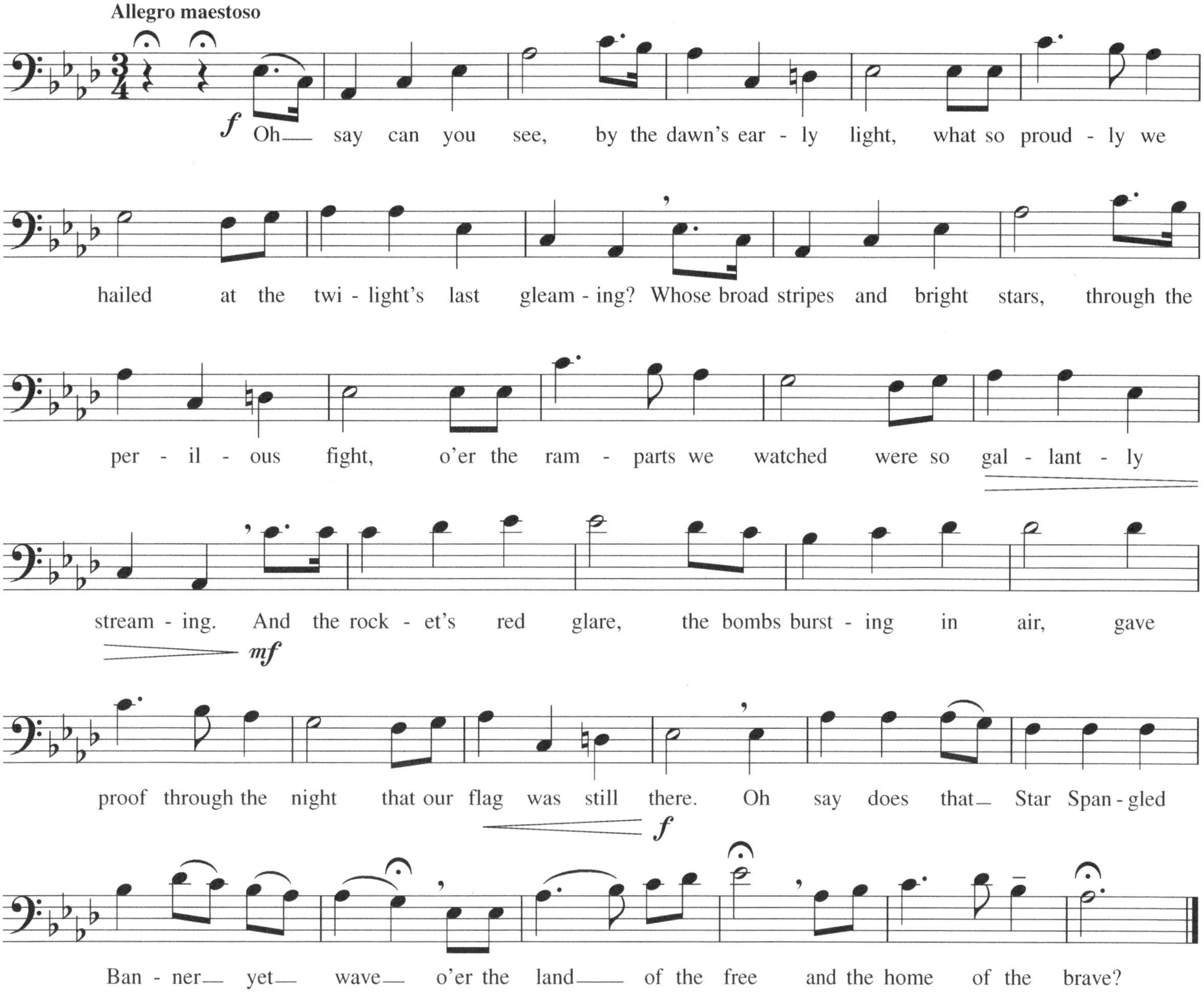

Allegro maestoso
f
Oh say can you see, by the dawn's ear - ly light, what so proud - ly we
hailed at the twi - light's last gleam - ing? Whose broad stripes and bright stars, through the
per - il - ous fight, o'er the ram - parts we watched were so gal - lant - ly
stream - ing. And the rock - et's red glare, the bombs burst - ing in air, gave
mf
proof through the night that our flag was still there. Oh say does that Star Span - gled
f
Ban - ner yet wave o'er the land of the free and the home of the brave?

THEORY

Dynamics

pp – *pianissimo* (play very softly) ***ff*** – *fortissimo* (play very loudly)
Remember to use full breath support to produce the best possible tone and intonation.

73. INTERMEZZO

1.
mf
p
2.
pp
f
ff

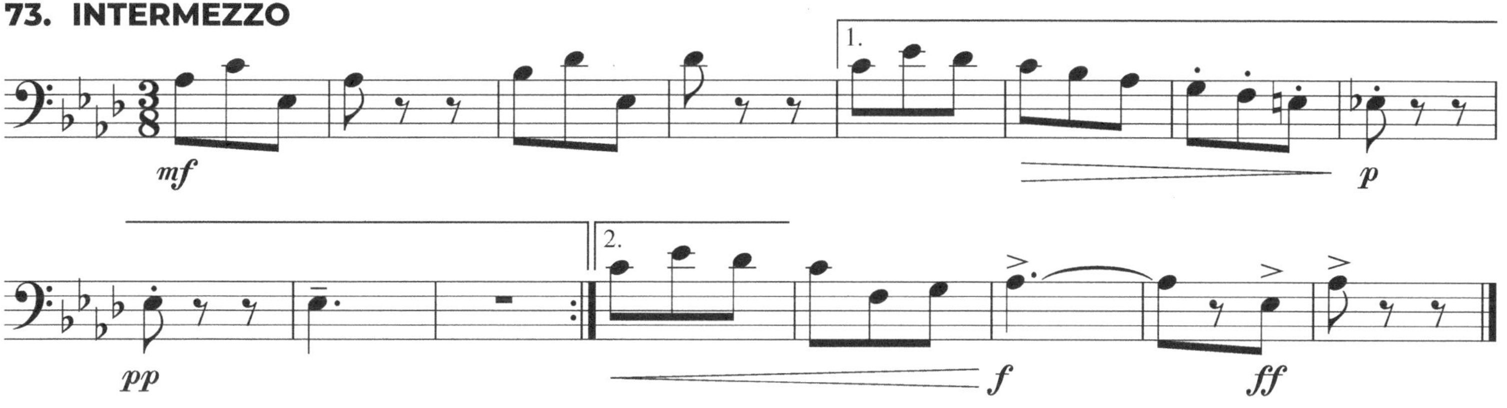

74. RHYTHM RAP

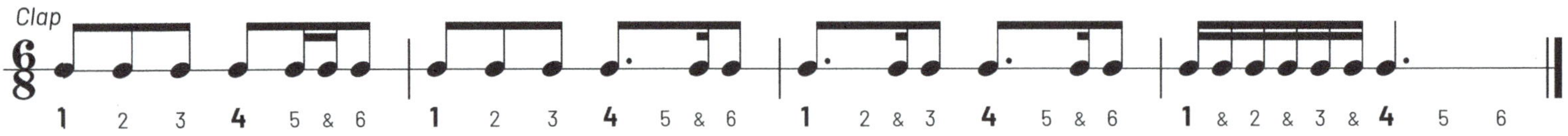
Clap
1 2 3 4 5 & 6
1 2 3 4 5 & 6
1 2 & 3 4 5 & 6
1 & 2 & 3 & 4 5 6

75. MORNING STAR

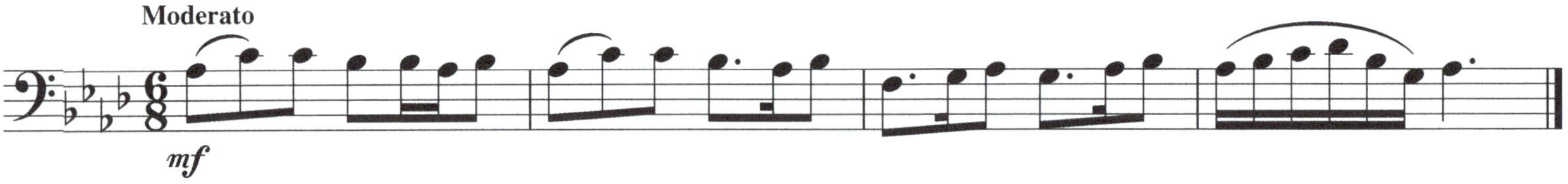
Moderato
mf

76. SONATA

Wolfgang Amadeus Mozart

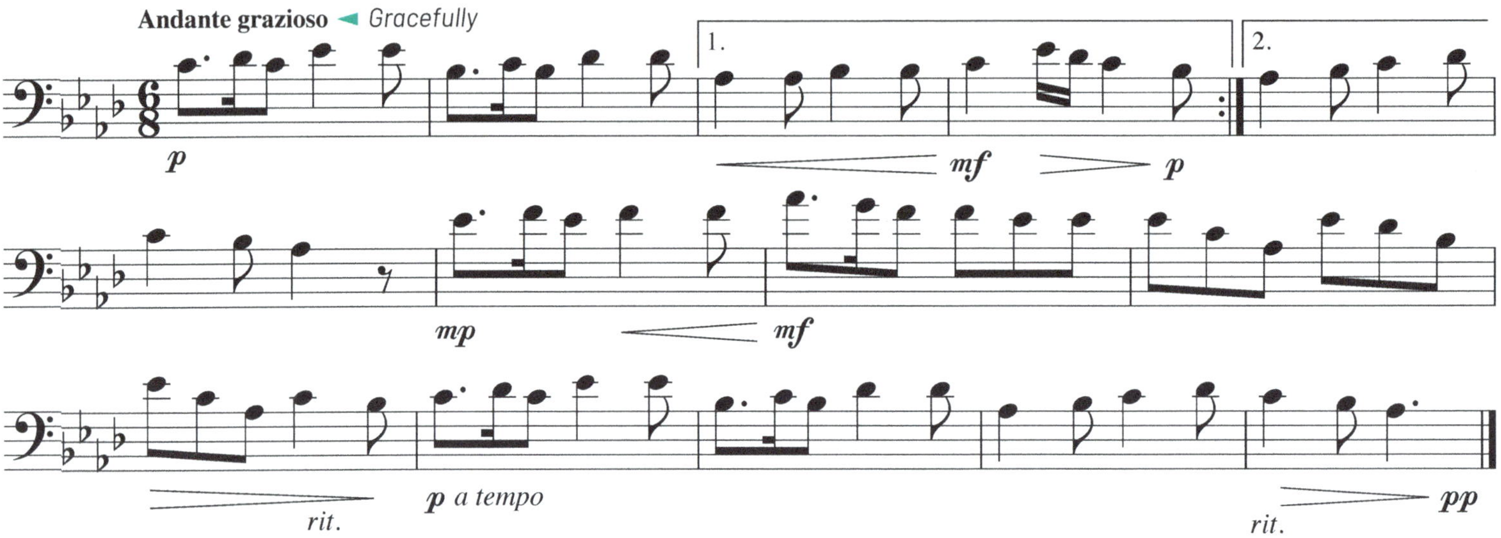
Andante grazioso ◄ Gracefully
p
1.
mf
p
2.
mp
mf
rit.
p a tempo
rit.
pp

77. RONDEAU

Jean-Joseph Mouret

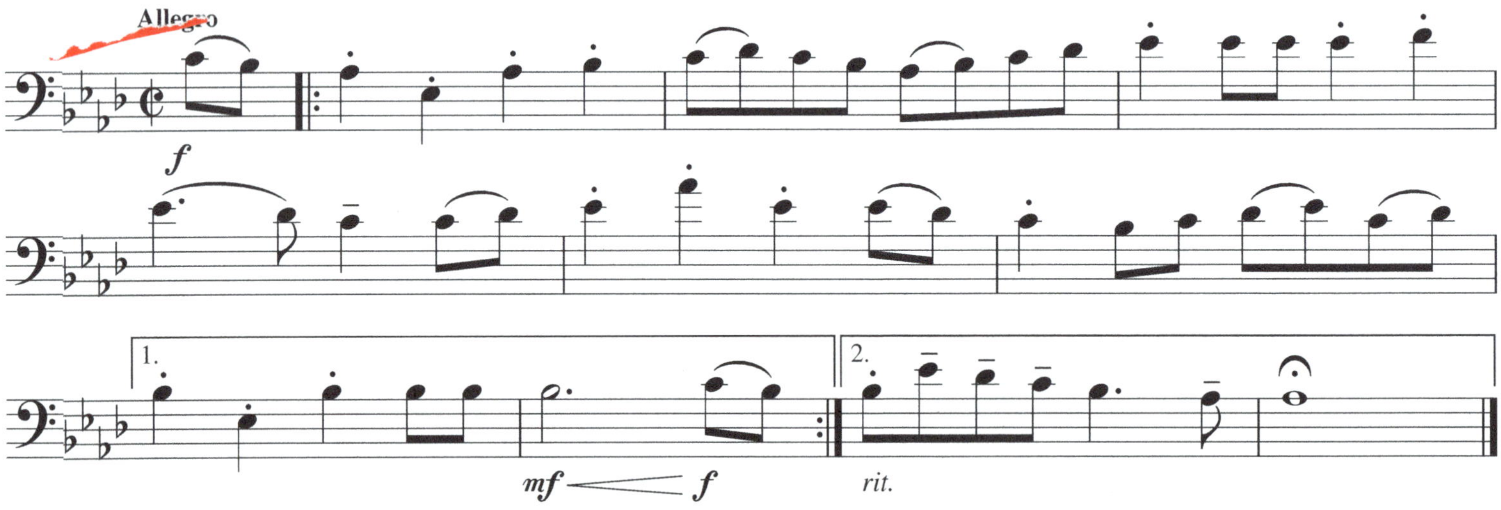
Allegro
f
1.
mf
f
2.
rit.

THEORY

Grace Note A small note (or notes) which is played on, or slightly before the beat.

78. JULIET'S WALTZ

Charles Gounod

Tempo di valse
mf
f

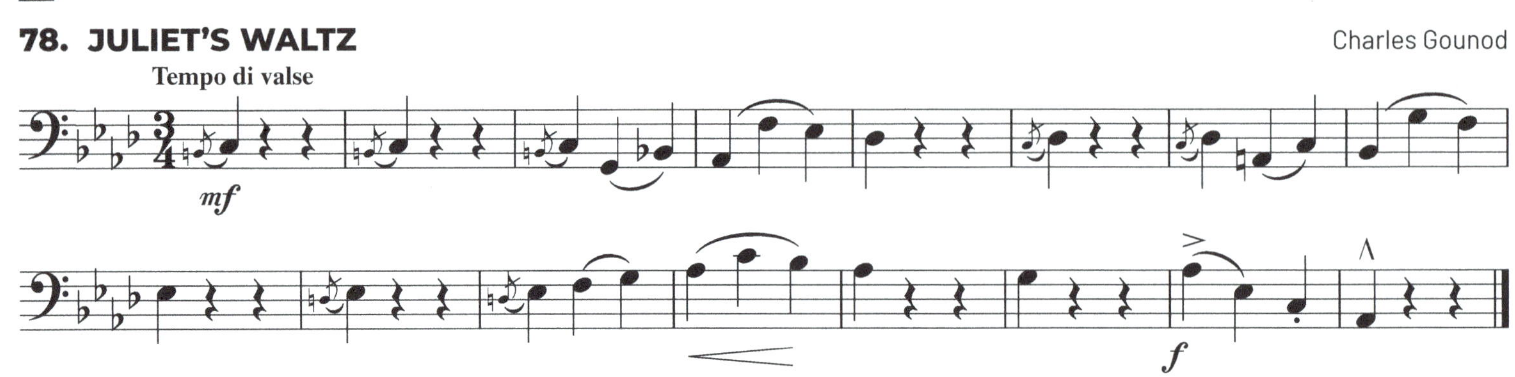

F MINOR

79. NATURAL MINOR *Practice both upper and lower octaves.*

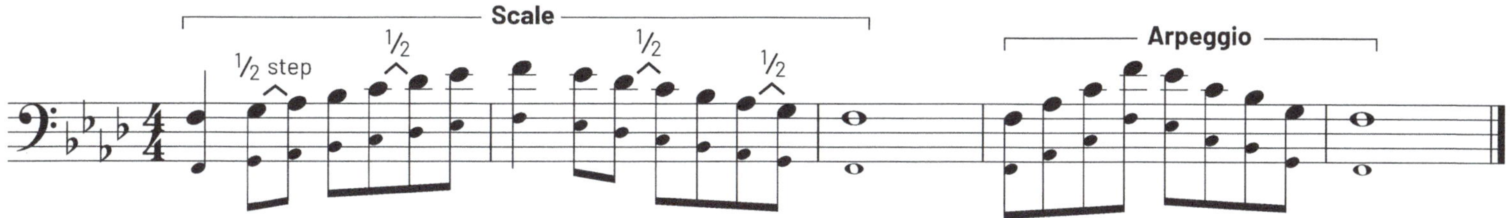

80. HARMONIC MINOR

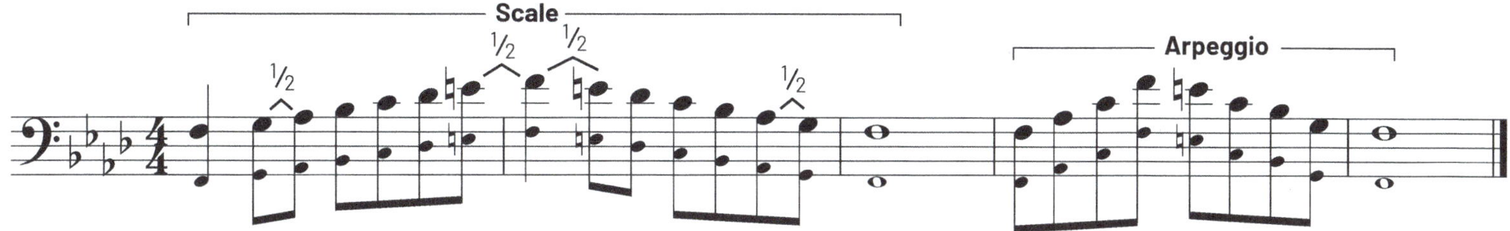

81. SORCERER'S APPRENTICE

Paul Dukas

Allegro agitato ◄ *Agitated*

82. I WALK THE ROAD AGAIN

American

83. ESSENTIAL ELEMENTS QUIZ – GREENSLEEVES

English Folk Song

C MAJOR

84. SCALE AND ARPEGGIO

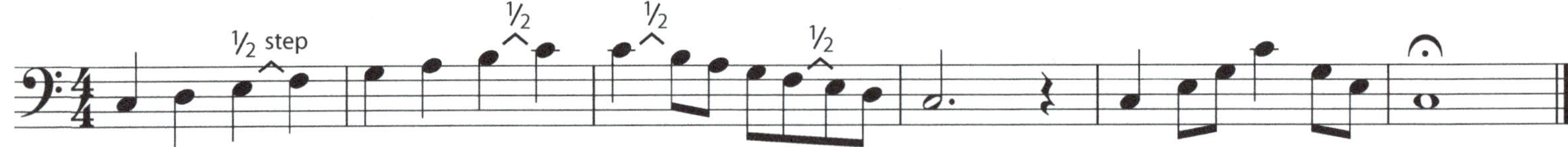

85. EXERCISE IN THIRDS

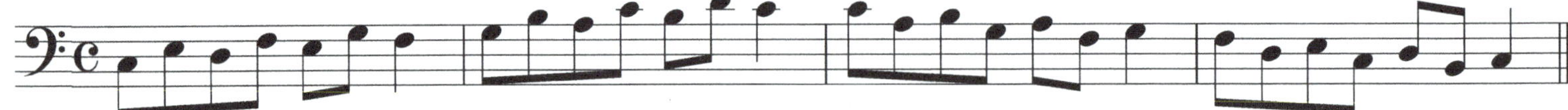

86. ARPEGGIO STUDY

87. TWO-PART ETUDE *Practice both upper and lower octaves.*

88. CHROMATIC SCALE

89. BALANCE BUILDER

90. CHORALE

African American spirituals originated in the 1700's. As one of the largest categories of true American folk music, these melodies were sung and passed on for generations without being written down. Black and white people worked together to publish the first spiritual collection in 1867, four years after *The Emancipation Proclamation* was signed into law.

91. SIT DOWN, SISTER

African American Spiritual

Allegro

f

Fine

mp

f

mp

f

D.S. al Fine

92. SPINNING SONG – Duet

Johann Ellmenreich

Moderato

A 2

B 2

mf

mf

Fine

p *cresc.*

p *cresc.*

THEORY

Quarter Note Triplets

Similar to eighth note triplets where 1 beat is divided into 3 equal notes,

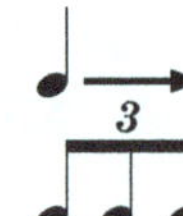

quarter note triplets divide 2 beats into 3 equal notes.

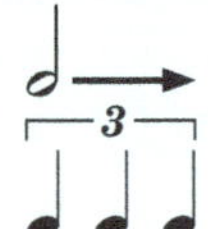

93. RHYTHM RAP

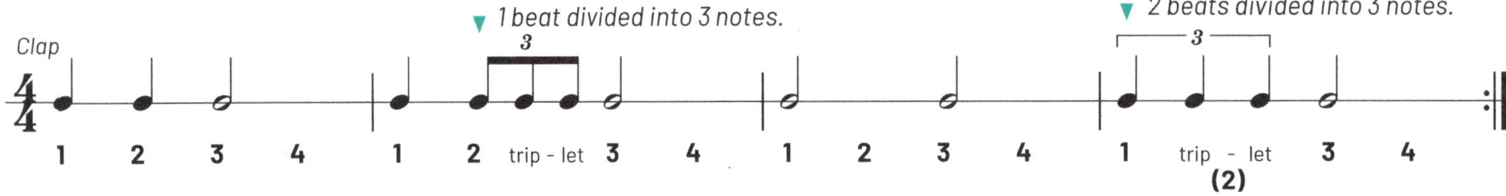

94. THREE FOR TWO

95. SURIRAM'S SONG

Malaysian Folk Song

HISTORY

Africa is a large continent that is made up of many nations, and **African folk music** is as diverse as its many cultures. Folk songs from any country are expressions of work, love, war, sadness, and joy. This song is from Tanzania. The words describe a rabbit hopping and running through a field. Listen to the percussion section play African-sounding drums and rhythms.

96. JIBULI (The Rabbit's Song)

Adapted Tanzanian Folk Song

A MINOR

97. NATURAL MINOR

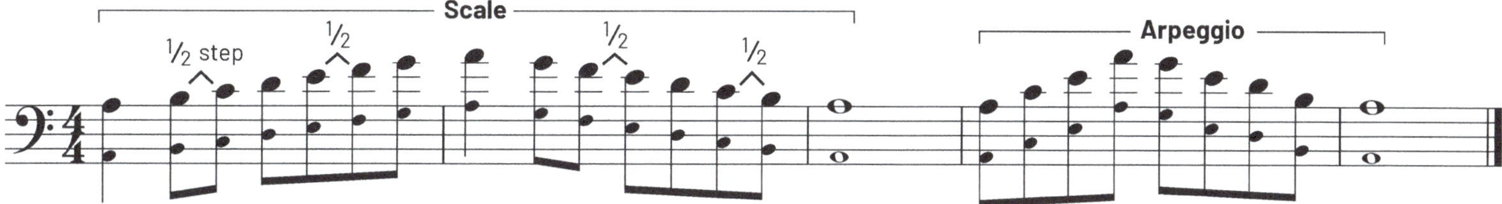

98. HARMONIC MINOR

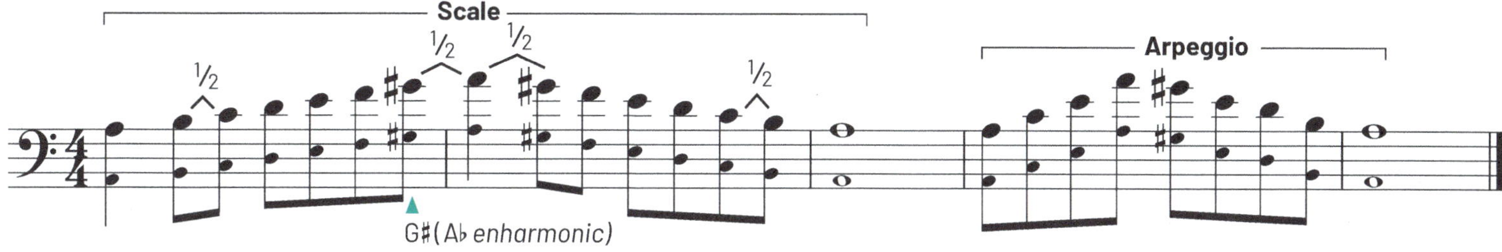

Meter Changes

THEORY

Meter changes, or changing time signatures within a section of music, are commonly found in contemporary music. Composers use this technique to create a unique rhythm, pulse, or musical style.

99. TIME ZONES

HISTORY

Important French composers of the late 19th century include **Claude Debussy** (1862–1918), **Gabriel Fauré** (1845–1924), **Erik Satie** (1866–1925), **César Franck** (1822–1890), **Camille Saint-Saëns** (1835–1921), and **Paul Dukas** (1865–1935). Their works continue to have influence on the music of modern day composers. Gabriel Fauré wrote *Pavanne* (originally for orchestra) in 1887, two years before the Eiffel Tower was completed in Paris.

100. PAVANNE

Gabriel Fauré

Andante espressivo

mp

rit.

pp

D♭ MAJOR

101. SCALE AND ARPEGGIO

102. EXERCISE IN THIRDS

103. ARPEGGIO STUDY

104. TWO-PART ETUDE

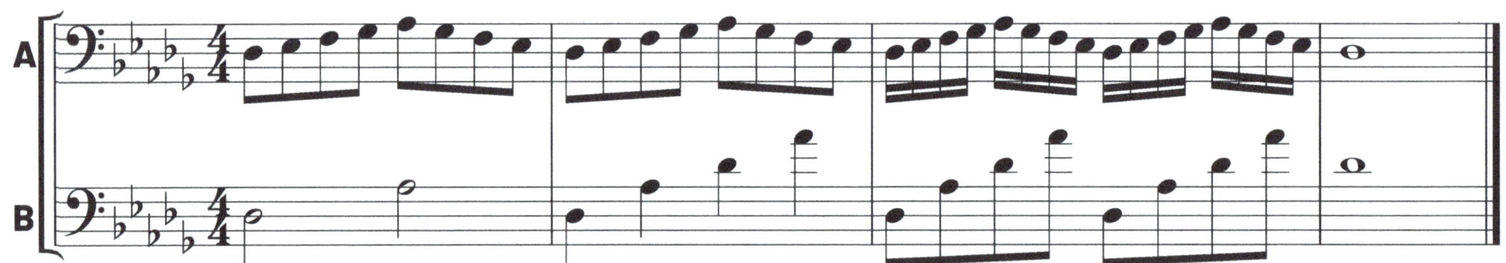

105. CHROMATIC SCALE

106. BALANCE BUILDER

107. CHORALE

108. GERMAN NATIONAL ANTHEM

Franz Josef Haydn

Maestoso

mf

f

109. JOY

Johann Sebastian Bach

Andante espressivo ◄ *Expressively*

mp

rit.

5/4 Time Signature

= **5 beats** per measure
= **Quarter** note gets one beat

Conducting

Practice conducting these five-beat patterns.

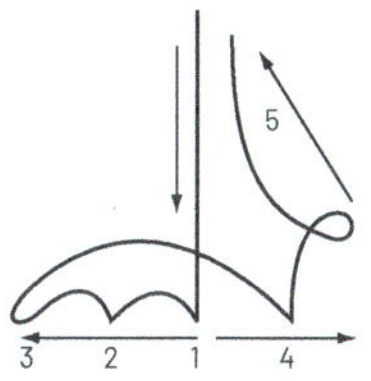

3 2 1 4 5 or 2 1 3 4 5

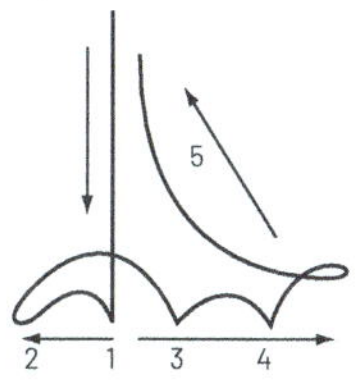

THEORY

110. RHYTHM RAP

Clap

1 2 & 3 4 5 1 2 3 4 5

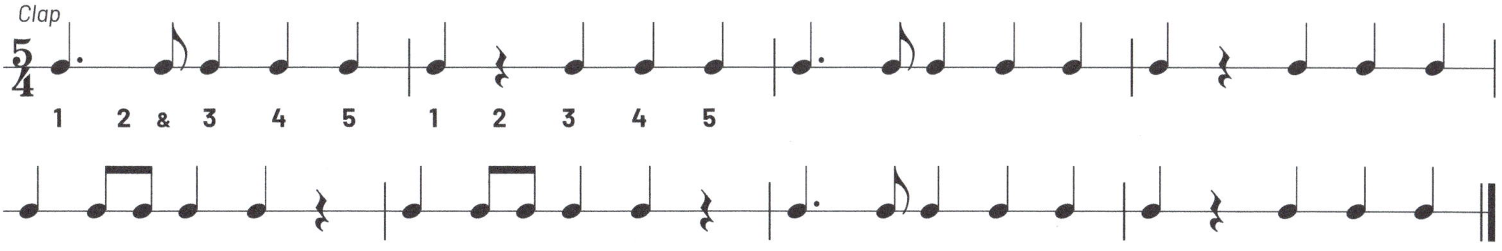

111. LET'S COUNT FIVE

Moderato

mf

sfz

112. SUKURU ITO

African Folk Song

HISTORY

English composer **George Frideric Handel** (1685–1759) lived during the **Baroque Period (1600–1750)**. *Water Music* was written in honor of England's King George I. The first performance took place on the Thames River on July 17, 1717. Fifty musicians performed the work while floating on a barge. Handel lived during the same time as Johann Sebastian Bach, perhaps the most famous Baroque composer.

113. WATER MUSIC

George Frideric Handel

114. ESSENTIAL TECHNIQUE QUIZ – PICTURES AT AN EXHIBITION

Modeste Mussorgsky

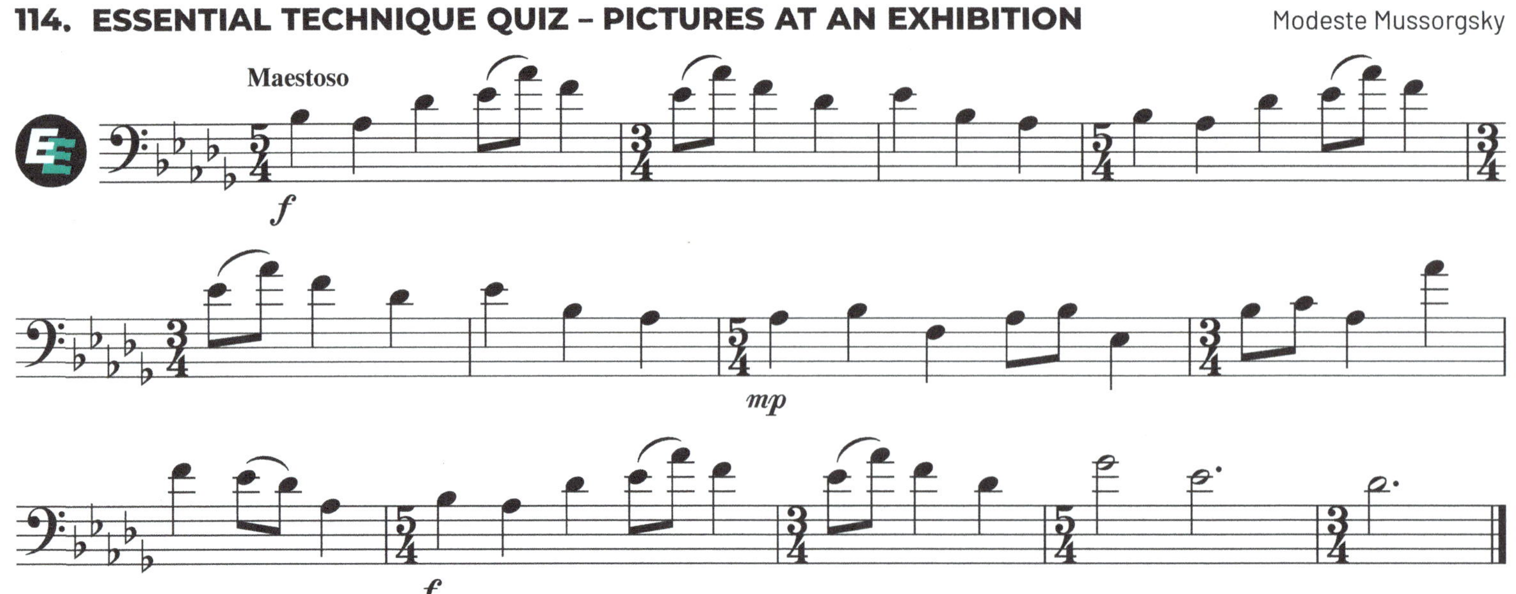

B♭ MINOR

115. NATURAL MINOR

116. HARMONIC MINOR

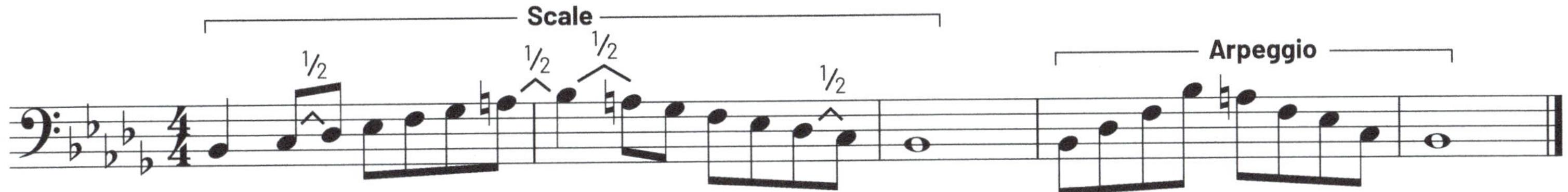

THEORY

Ostinato A clear and distinct musical phrase that is repeated persistently.

HISTORY

British composer **Gustav Holst** (1874–1934) is one of the most widely played composers for concert band today. Many of his compositions, including his familiar military suites, are based on tuneful English folk songs. His most famous work for orchestra, *The Planets* (1916), has seven movements—one written for each known planet, excluding Earth.

117. MARS – Duet/Trio

Gustav Holst

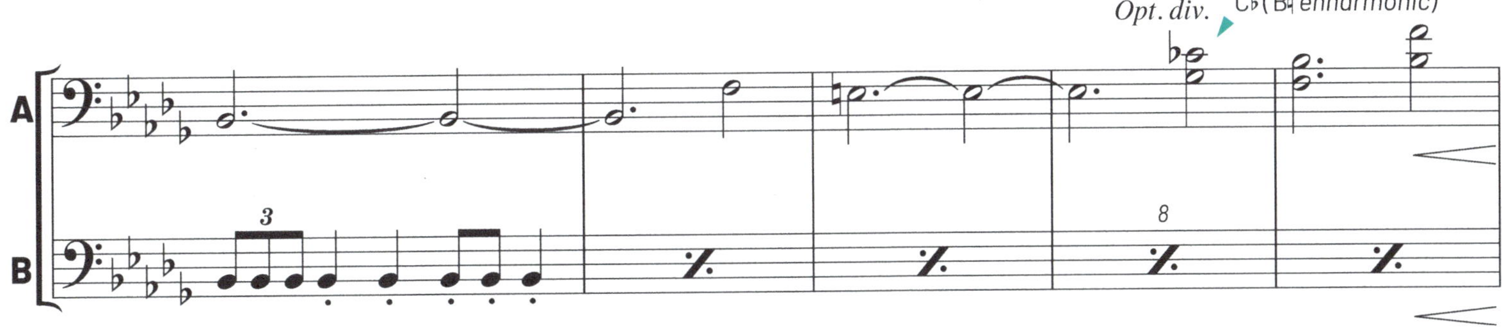

G MAJOR

118. SCALE AND ARPEGGIO *Practice both upper and lower octaves.*

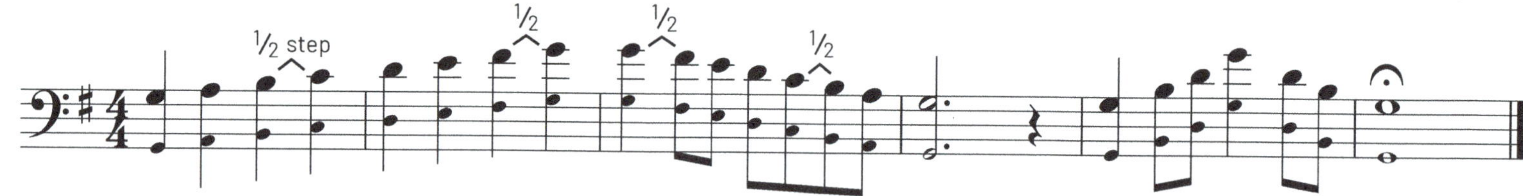

119. EXERCISE IN THIRDS

120. ARPEGGIO STUDY

121. TWO-PART ETUDE

122. CHROMATIC SCALE

123. BALANCE BUILDER

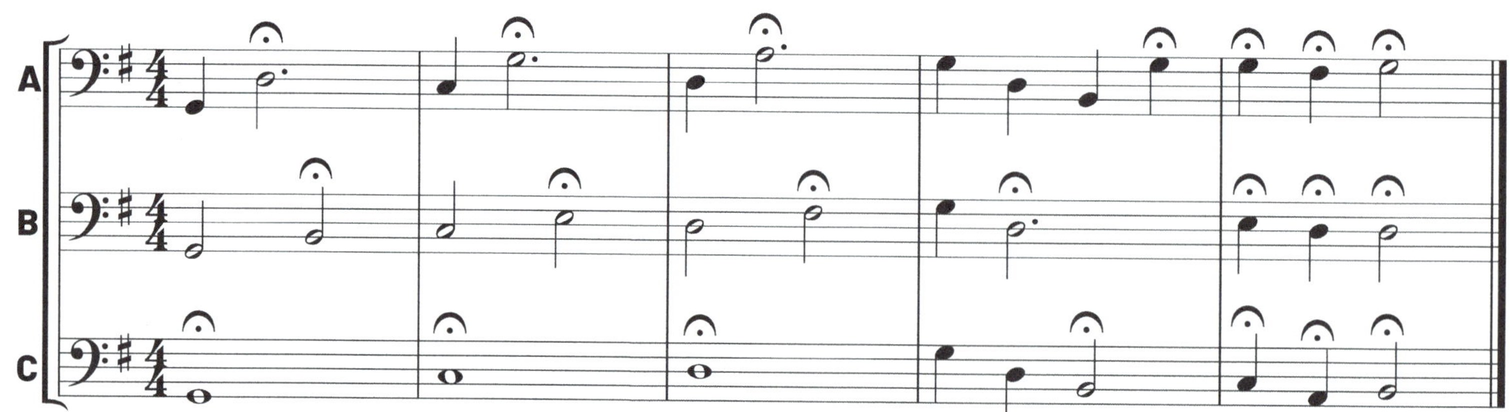

124. CHORALE

Norwegian composer **Edvard Grieg** (1843–1907) based much of his music on the folk songs and dances of Norway. During the late 19th century, composers often used melodies from their native land. This trend is called **nationalism**. Russian **Modeste Mussorgsky** (1839–1881), Czech **Antonin Dvořák** (1841–1904), and Englishman **Sir Edward Elgar** (1857–1934) are other famous composers whose music was influenced by nationalism.

125. NORWEGIAN DANCE

Edvard Grieg

126. FRENCH NATIONAL ANTHEM (LA MARSEILLAISE)

Rouget De L'Isle

Music written during the **Renaissance Period (1430–1600)** was often upbeat and dance-like. *Wolsey's Wilde* was originally written for the lute, an ancestor to the guitar and the most popular instrument of the Renaissance era. Modern day concert band composer Gordon Jacob used this popular song in his *William Byrd Suite*, written as a tribute to English composer William Byrd (1543–1623).

127. WOLSEY'S WILDE

Anonymous

Animato ◄ *Animated, lively*

E MINOR

128. NATURAL MINOR *Practice both upper and lower octaves.*

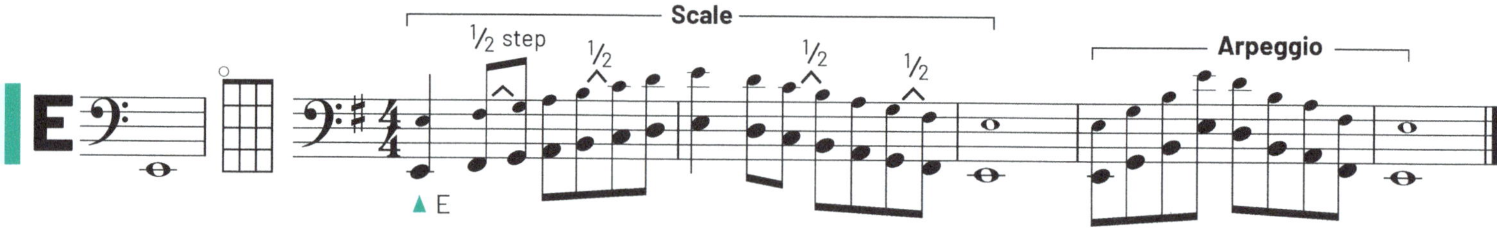

129. HARMONIC MINOR

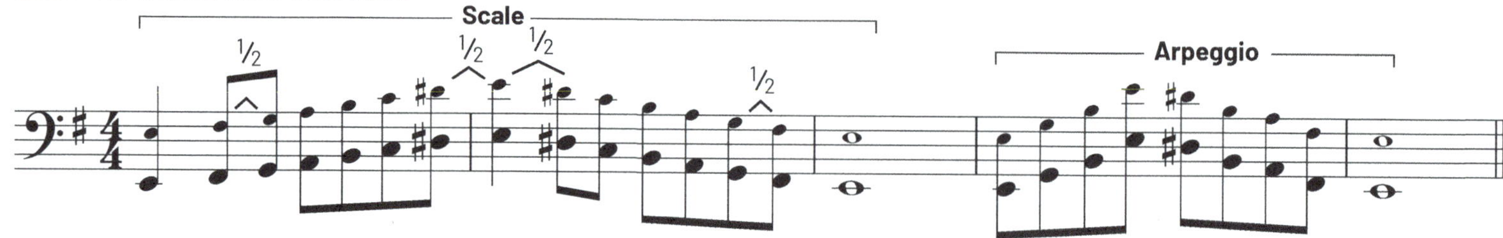

HISTORY

Native Japanese instruments include the *shakuhachi*, a bamboo flute played pointing downward; the *koto*, a long zither with movable frets played sitting down; and the *gakubiwa*, a pear-shaped lute with strings that are plucked. These instruments have been an important part of Japanese culture since the 8th century. *Kabuki*, a Japanese theatrical form that originated in 1603, remains popular in Japan. Performers play native Japanese instruments during Kabuki performances.

130. SONG OF THE SHAKUHACHI

Japanese Folk Song

THEORY

D.C. al Coda At the **D.C. al Coda**, play again from the beginning to the indication **To Coda** ⊕, then skip to the section marked ⊕ **Coda**, meaning "ending section."

D.S. al Coda Similar to **D.C. al Coda**, but return to the sign 𝄋.

131. POLOVETZIAN DANCES

Alexander Borodin

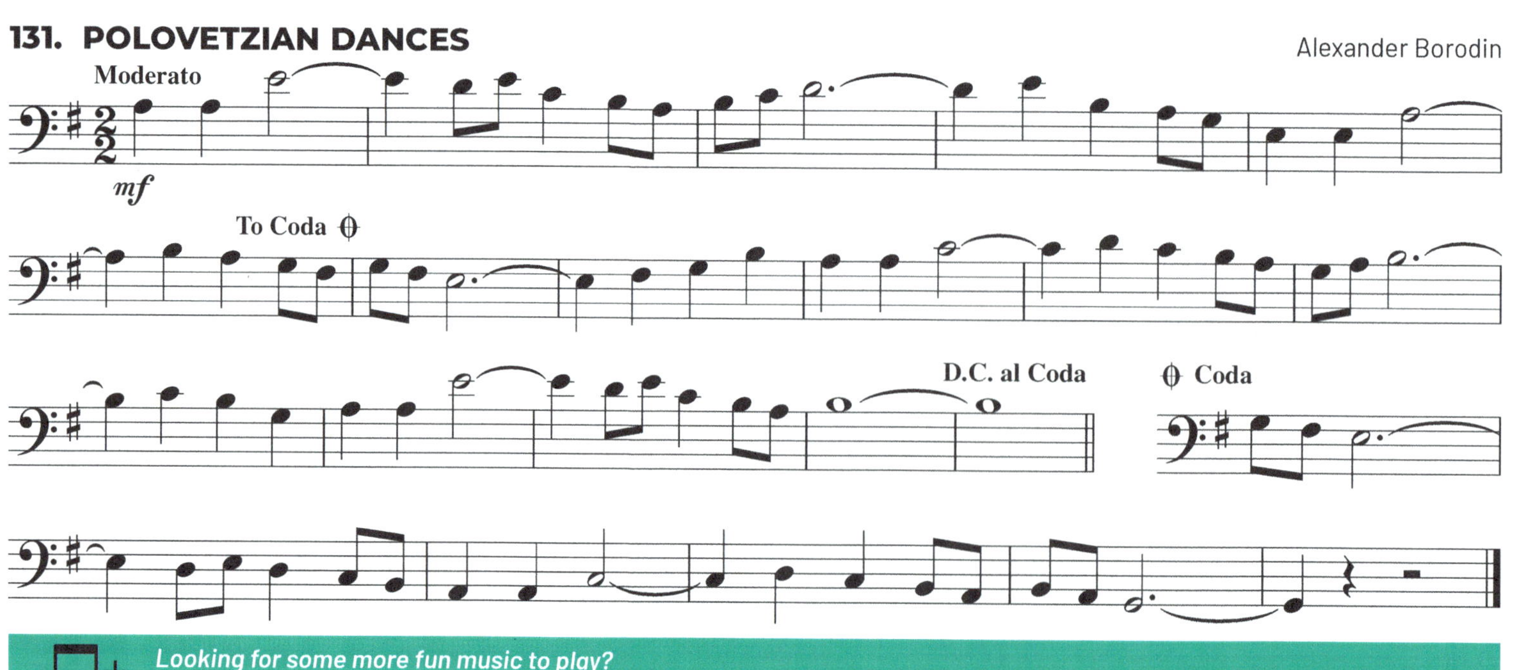

Looking for some more fun music to play?
See the inside front cover for instructions on accessing recent popular Bonus Songs.

D MAJOR

132. SCALE AND ARPEGGIO

133. EXERCISE IN THIRDS

134. ARPEGGIO STUDY

135. TWO-PART ETUDE

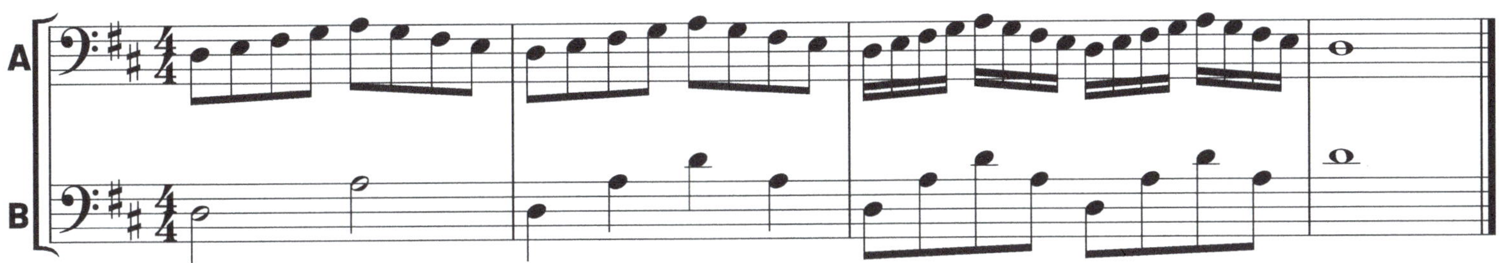

136. CHORALE

B MINOR

137. NATURAL MINOR

138. HARMONIC MINOR

HISTORY

Latin American music combines the folk music from South and Central America, the Caribbean Islands, American Indian, Spanish, and Portuguese cultures. Melodies are often accompanied by drums, maracas, and claves. Latin American music continues to influence jazz, classical, and popular styles of music. *Cielito Lindo* is a Latin American love song.

139. CIELITO LINDO

C. Fernandez

HISTORY

Tchaikovsky, along with Wagner, Brahms, Mendelssohn, and Chopin, helped define the musical era known as the **Romantic Period (1825–1900)**. The "symphonic tone poem" from this period continues to be one of the most popular musical forms performed by orchestras and bands today.

140. WALTZ IN FIVE (from SYMPHONY NO. 6)

Peter I. Tchaikovsky

mf

141. THE YOUNG CHEVALIER

Scottish

f

To Coda

D.S. al Coda

Coda

G♭ MAJOR

142. SCALE AND ARPEGGIO *Practice both upper and lower octaves.*

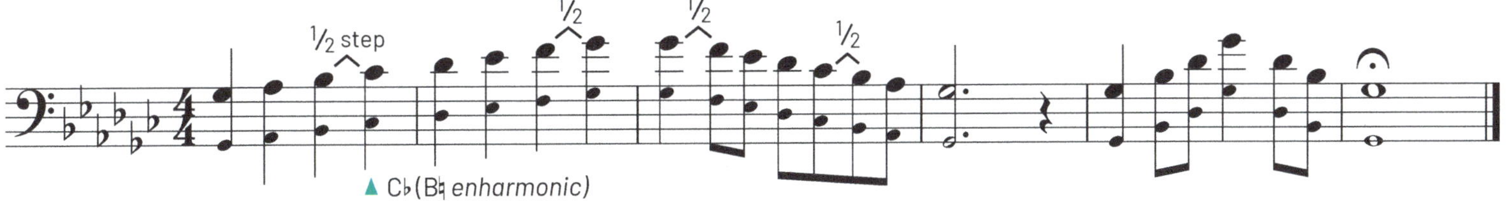

143. EXERCISE IN THIRDS

144. ARPEGGIO STUDY

145. TWO-PART ETUDE

146. CHORALE

E♭ MINOR

147. NATURAL MINOR

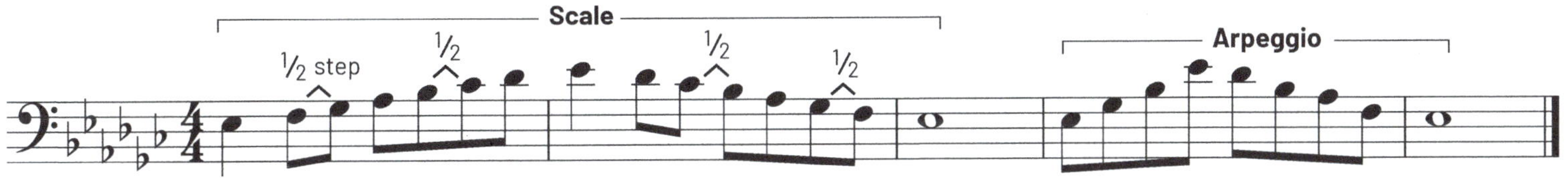

148. HARMONIC MINOR

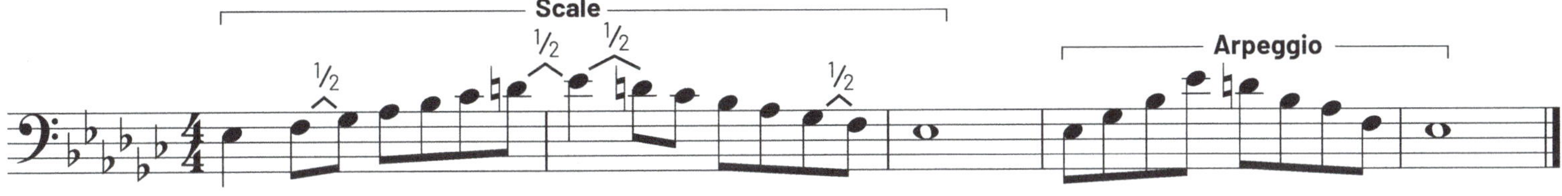

INDIVIDUAL STUDY – Electric Bass

149. STUDY IN C MAJOR

150. LEGATO STUDY

151. STACCATO ETUDE

152. ARTICULATION STUDY

153. CHROMATIC CHALLENGE NO. 1

INDIVIDUAL STUDY – Electric Bass

154. CHROMATIC CHALLENGE NO. 2

155. 16TH NOTE PATTERNS AND ARTICULATION

156. EXERCISE IN 12/8

157. TRIPLET WORKOUT

READING SKILL BUILDERS

158. READING SKILL BUILDER NO. 1

159. READING SKILL BUILDER NO. 2

160. READING SKILL BUILDER NO. 3

161. READING SKILL BUILDER NO. 4

162. READING SKILL BUILDER NO. 5

READING SKILL BUILDERS

163. READING SKILL BUILDER NO. 6

164. READING SKILL BUILDER NO. 7

165. READING SKILL BUILDER NO. 8

166. READING SKILL BUILDER NO. 9

167. CHORALE (Prelude from Hansel and Gretel)

Engelbert Humperdinck
Arr. by John Higgins

168. CHORALE (Based on a Theme by Palestrina)

Arr. by John Higgins

169. CHORALE (Based on a Theme by J. S. Bach)

Arr. by John Higgins

170. CHORALE (Based on a Theme by Tchaikovsky)
Arr. by John Higgins
Broadly
mp
5
10
rall.
171. CHORALE (Erhalt Uns In Der Wahrheit)
Johann Sebastian Bach
Arr. by John Higgins
Andante
mf
5
9
13
rit.
172. CHORALE (Navy Hymn)
John Dykes
Arr. by John Higgins
Andante
mp
p
5
9
cresc.
mf rall.
173. CHORALE (Prelude)
Frederic Chopin
Arr. by John Higgins
Adagio
f
p

RHYTHM STUDIES

1 2 3 4

5 6 7 8

9 10 11 12

13 14 15 16

17 18 19 20

21 22 23 24

25 26 27 28 29 30 31 32

33 34 35 36 37 38 39 40

41 42 43 44 45 46 47 48

49 50 51 52 53 54 55 56

RHYTHM STUDIES

THE BASICS OF JAZZ STYLE from Essential Elements for Jazz Ensemble

Accenting "2 and 4"

For most traditional music the important beats in 4/4 time are 1 and 3. In jazz, however, the emphasis is usually on beats 2 and 4. Emphasizing "2 and 4" gives the music a jazz feeling.

174. ACCENTING 2 AND 4

Jazz Articulations

There are four basic articulations in jazz.

Swing 8th Notes Sound Different Than They Look

In swing, the 2nd 8th note of each beat is actually played like the last third of a triplet, and slightly accented. 8th notes in swing style are usually played *legato*.

175. SWING 8TH NOTES

Quarter Notes

Quarter notes in swing style are usually played detached (*staccato*) with accents on beats 2 and 4.

176. QUARTERS AND 8THS

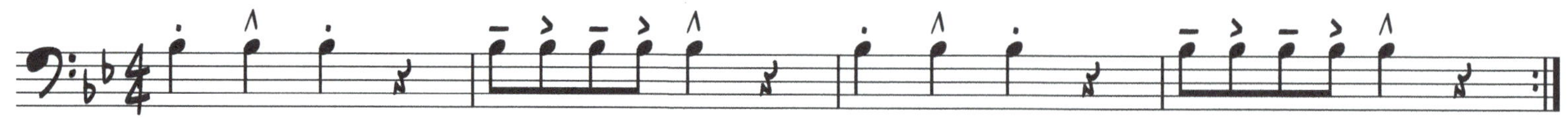

177. RUNNIN' AROUND

Syncopation in Jazz

When beats are played early (anticipated) or played late (delayed), the music becomes syncopated. Syncopation makes the music sound "jazzy."

178. WHEN THE SAINTS GO MARCHING IN – Without Syncopation

James Black and Katherine Purvis

179. WHEN THE SAINTS GO MARCHING IN – With Syncopation

"Jazzin' Up" the Melody by Adding Rhythms

Adding rhythms to a melody is another easy way to improvise in a jazz style. Start by filling out long notes with repeated 8th and quarter notes. Remember to swing the 8th notes (play *legato* and give the upbeats an accent).

180. "JAZZIN' UP" JINGLE BELLS

J. Pierpont

Original Melody

Walking Bass Line for Jazzed Up Melody

MAKE UP YOUR OWN (IMPROVISE)

181. LONDON BRIDGE

Original Melody

Walking Bass Line for Jazzed Up Melody

THEORY

Major Scales

Play major scales as part of your daily practice routine. Play all octaves, keys, and arpeggios at various dynamic levels and tempos. Keep a steady pulse. Try different articulation patterns, such as:

182. B♭ MAJOR

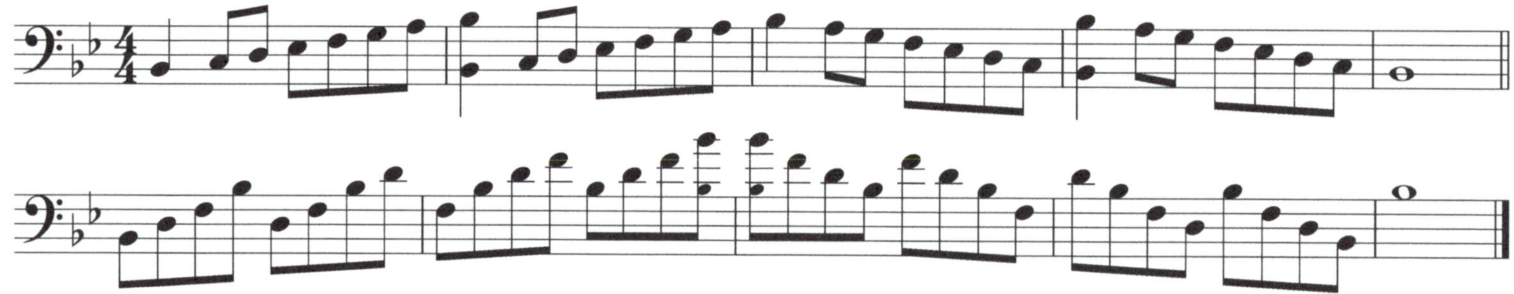

183. E♭ MAJOR

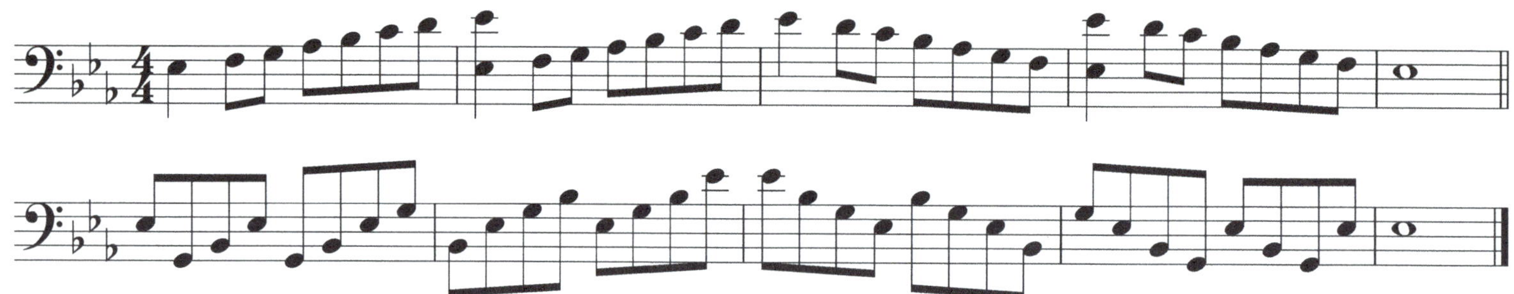

184. F MAJOR

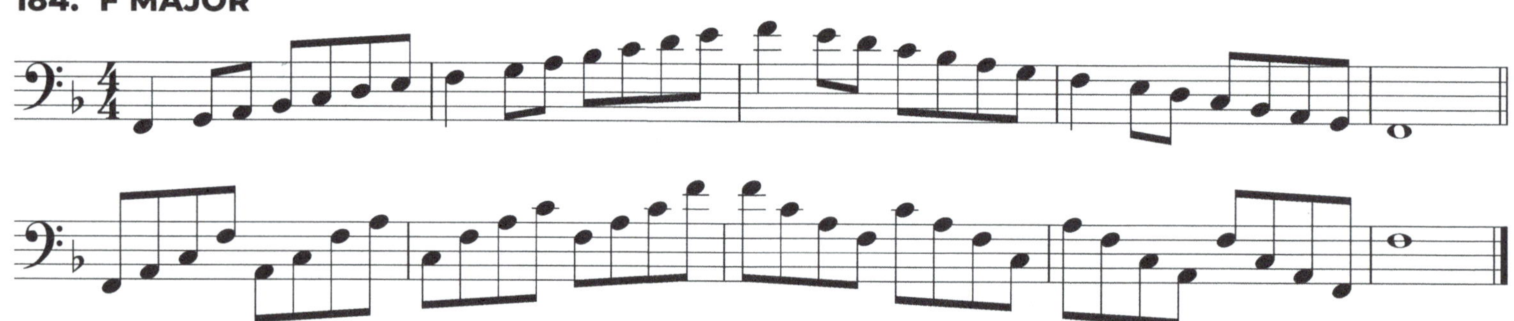

185. C MAJOR

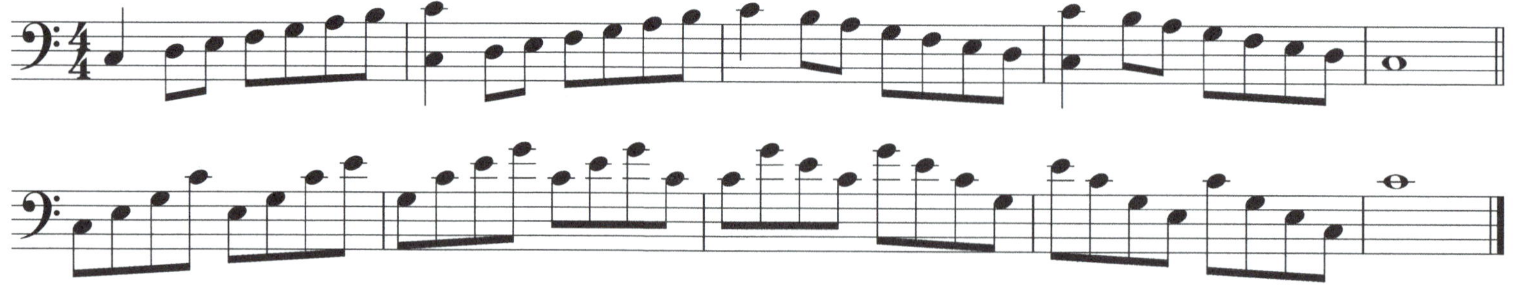

186. A♭ MAJOR

187. D♭ MAJOR

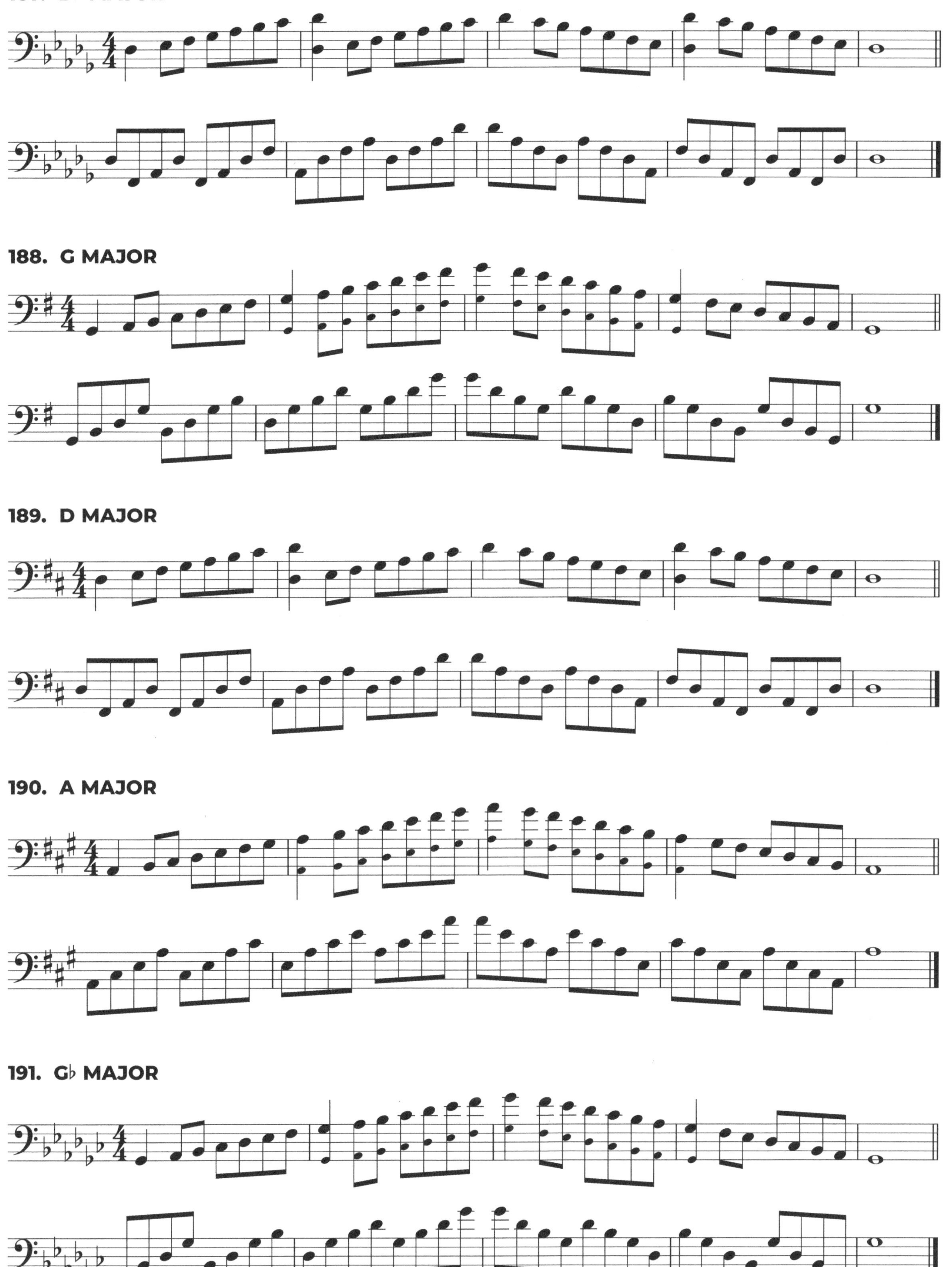

THEORY

Minor Scales

Play minor scales as part of your daily practice routine. Play all octaves, all three forms, and the arpeggios at various dynamic levels and tempos. Keep a steady pulse. Try different articulation patterns, such as:

192. D MINOR SCALE

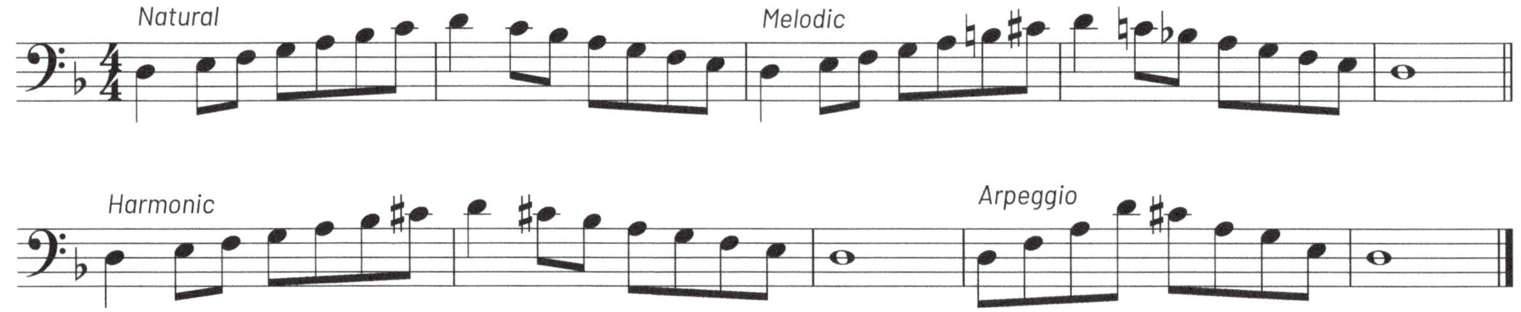

193. G MINOR SCALE

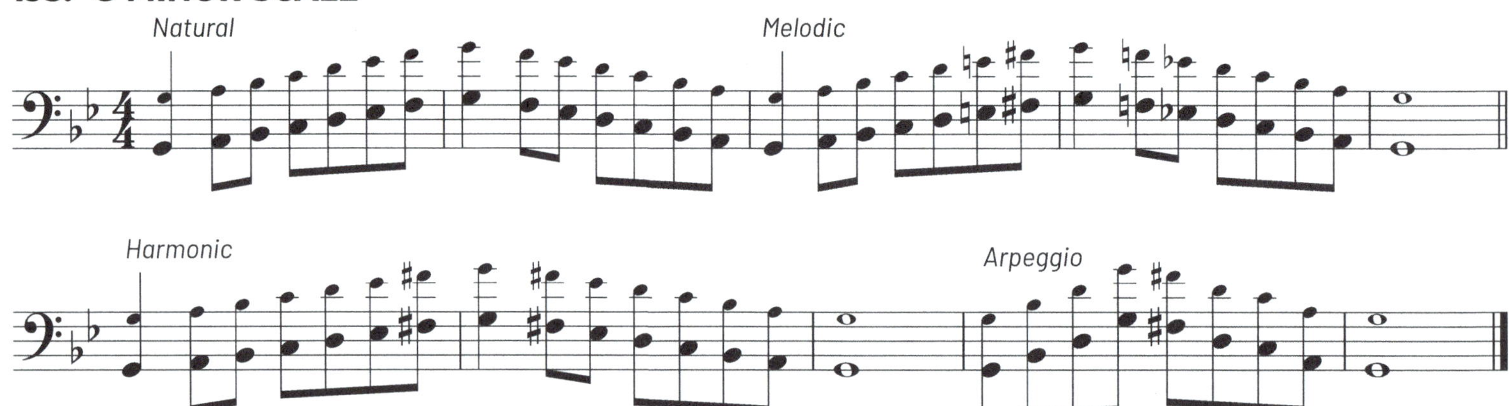

194. C MINOR SCALE

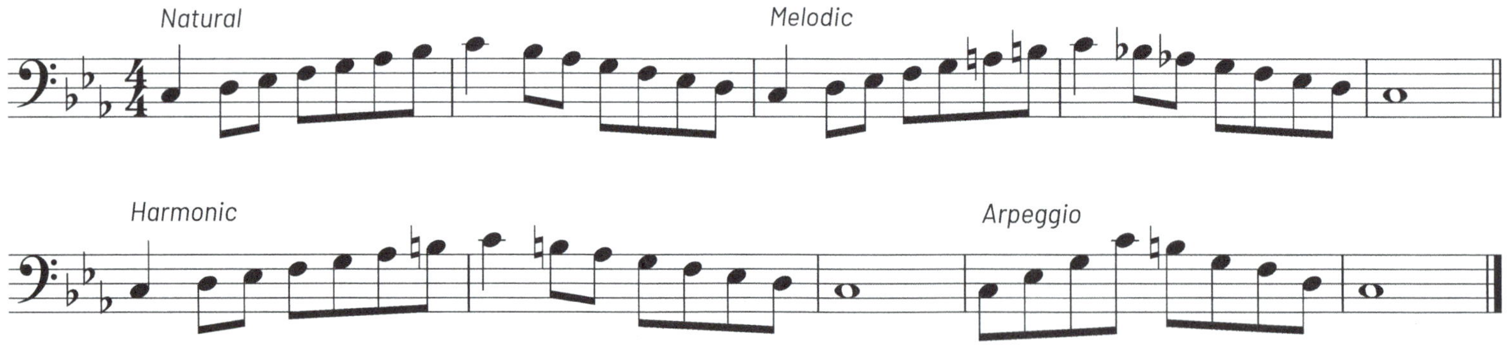

195. F MINOR SCALE

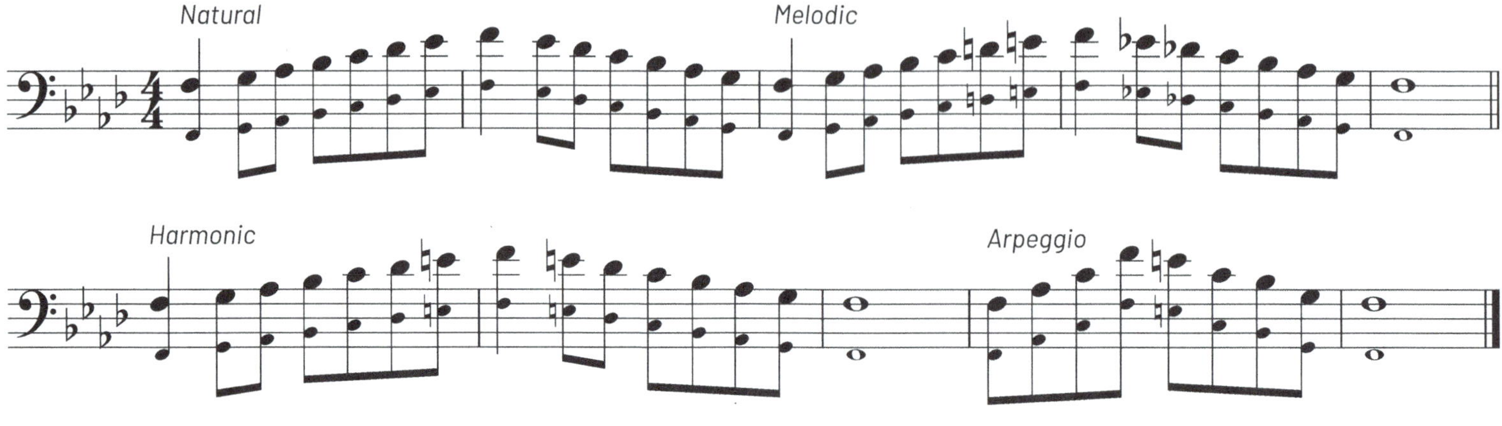

BASS TIPS

HOW TO CHANGE A STRING

If you're missing a string or your strings are old and need replacing, you'll need to know how to change them. The diagram below should help. Once you've inserted the ball-end of a string at the bridge, you need to wrap the other end around the tuning peg at the headstock. To do this, first insert the string in the posthole. Then, bend it sharply to hold it in place, and begin winding. You should allow enough slack to wrap the string around the peg 3 to 4 times; any excess can be removed with a good wire cutter.

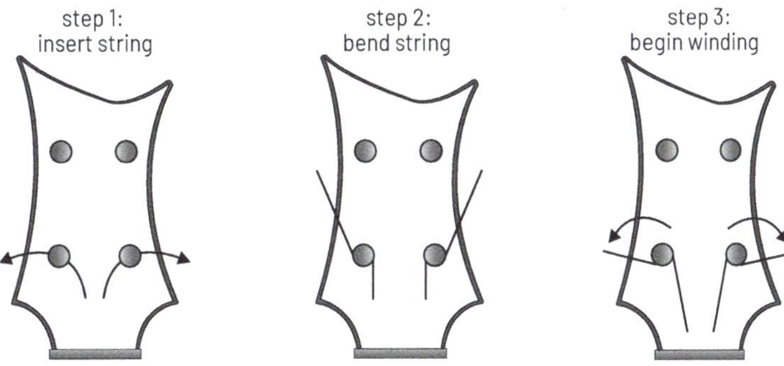

Keep in mind, new strings need to be stretched before you can expect them to hold their pitch. You can do this by playing on them awhile and tuning them up several times until each string remains in tune. (Lightly pulling on the strings one at a time, initially, can also help stretch them out.)

ADJUSTING THE BRIDGE

String height (or "action") can be adjusted by raising or lowering the bridge saddles of your bass. Some saddles require a small screwdriver, but most use a small Allen wrench, which can be purchased at a hardware store if one did not come with your bass at the time of purchase.

THE TRUSS ROD

Remember: your bass is wood (unless you purchased a graphite-neck model). With the changes of season come changes in your bass neck. Most basses have a steel rod through the neck, which can be adjusted to tighten or loosen neck tension. If you notice buzzing to be more frequent, it is a good idea to take your bass in to get the neck adjusted. If possible, watch how a professional does it so you can learn how to adjust the truss rod yourself.

FINGERING CHART

ELECTRIC BASS

Instrument Care Reminders

- Be sure your amplifier is turned off before plugging-in or unplugging the audio cable connecting it to your instrument.
- When unplugging a cable, hold it by the plug (not by the wire).
- After playing, wipe off the instrument and strings with a clean soft cloth. Return the instrument to its case.
- Close all the latches on your case when the instrument is inside.
- Keep all 4 strings in tune (at normal tension) to prevent warping of the neck.
- Your case is designed to hold only specific objects. If you force anything else into the case, it may damage your instrument.

strings

4th 3rd 2nd 1st

frets

1st 2nd 3rd 4th 5th

Fingerboard diagrams show where to play the notes. Circles are drawn on the diagram to indicate the fingers to be used to play the notes.

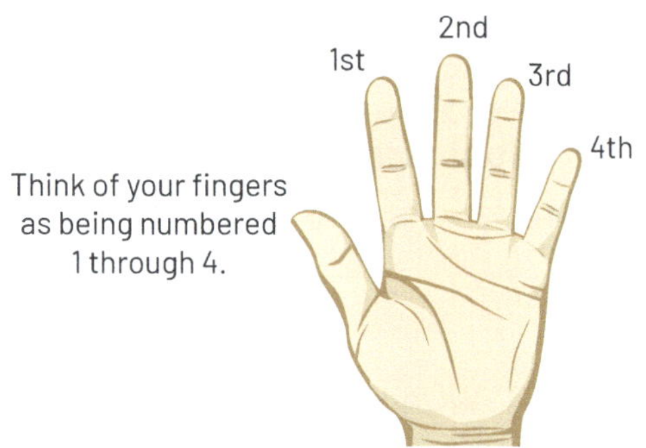

Instruments and photos courtesy of Yamaha.

E

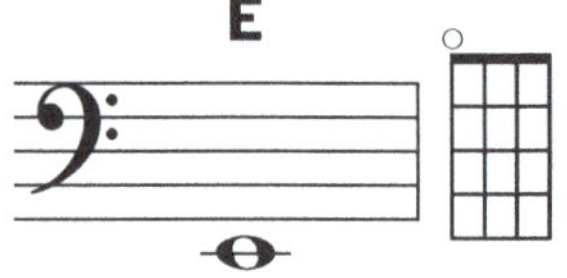

F

F♯ G♭

G

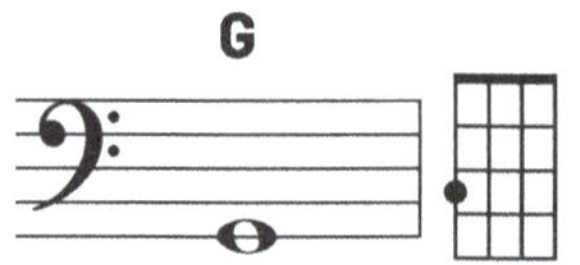

G♯ A♭

A

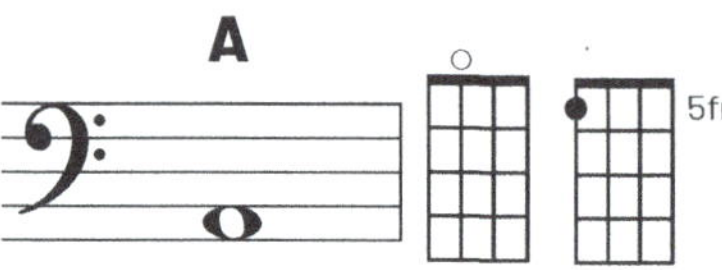

A♯ B♭

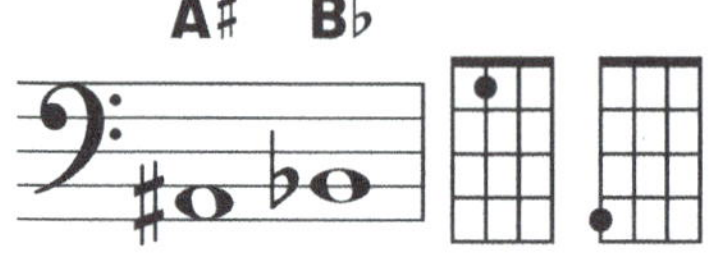

B

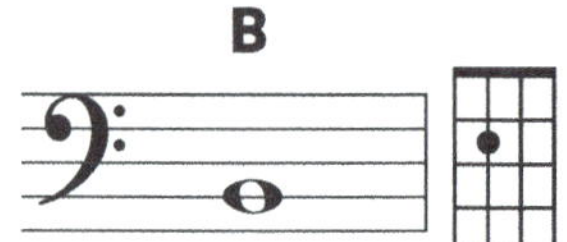

FINGERING CHART

ELECTRIC BASS

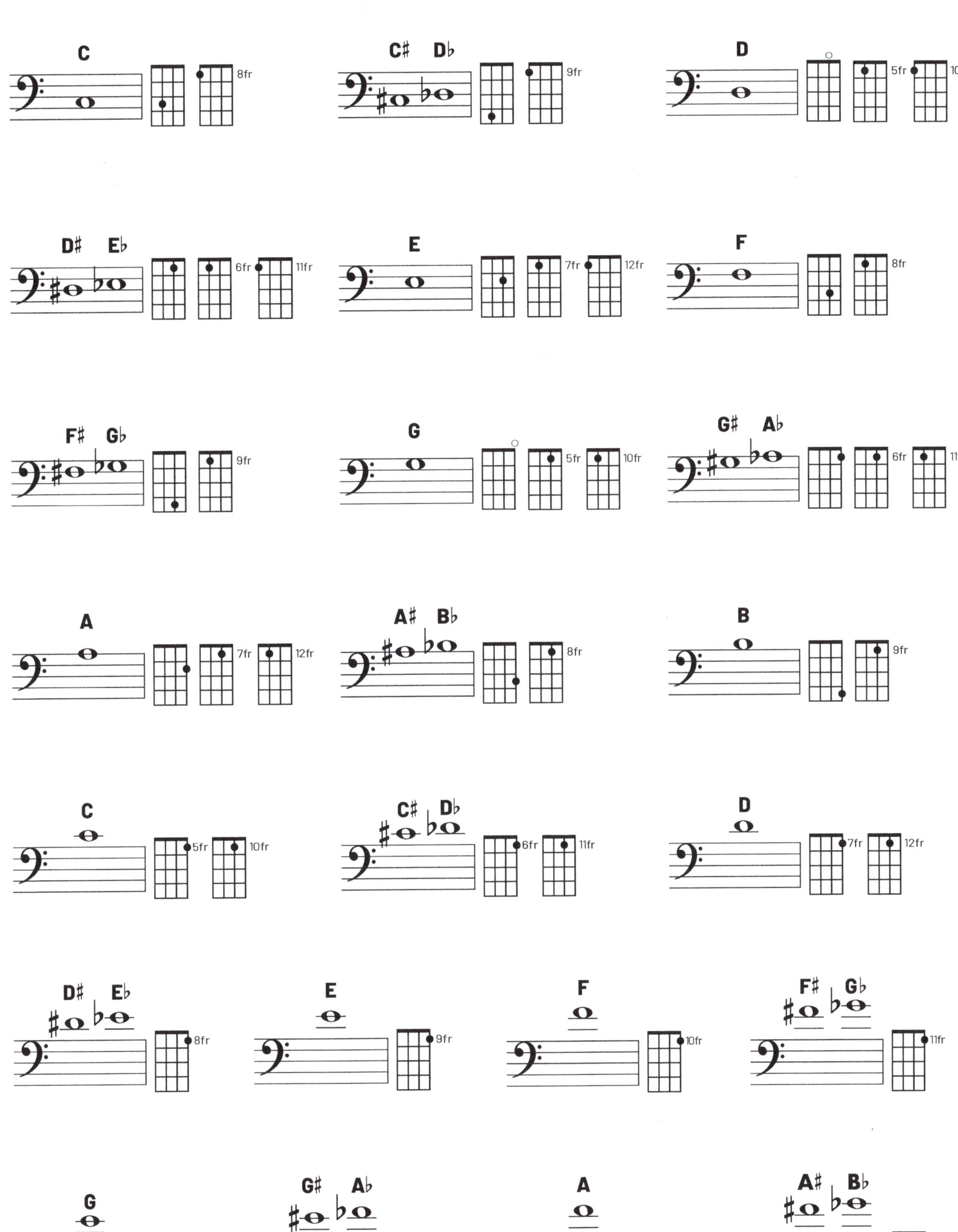

REFERENCE INDEX

Definitions (pg.)

Allegro Agitato 17
Allegro Marziale 27
Allegro Vivo 13
Andante Espressivo 23
Andante Grazioso 16
Animato 27
D.C. al Coda 28
D.S. al Coda 28
Divisi *(div.)* 2
Energetico 25
5/4 23
Fortissimo (***ff***) 15
Giocoso 11
Grace Note 16
Lento 8
Lento Mysterioso 9
Maestoso 3
Meter Changes 21
Minor Keys 5
Molto Rit. 8
9/8 4
Ostinato 25
Quarter Note Triplets 20
Pianissimo (***pp***) 15
16th Notes and Rests
in 6/8, 3/8, 9/8, 12/8 12
Tempo Di Valse 7
3/8 4
Triplets with Rests 11
12/8 8
Unison *(a2)* 2

Composers

JOHANN SEBASTIAN BACH
- Joy 23

ALEXANDER BORODIN
- Polovetzian Dances 28

CLAUDE DEBUSSY
- The Little Child 11

PAUL DUKAS
- Sorcerer's Apprentice 17

ANTONIN DVORÁK
- Slavonic Dance No. 2 13

JOHANN ELLMENREICH
- Spinning Song 19

GABRIEL FAURÉ
- Pavanne 21

CHARLES GOUNOD
- Juliet's Waltz 16

EDVARD GRIEG
- Norwegian Dance 27

GEORGE FRIDERIC HANDEL
- Hallelujah Chorus 3
- Sound an Alarm 3
- Water Music 24

FRANZ JOSEF HAYDN
- German National Anthem 23

GUSTAV HOLST
- Mars 25

JEAN-JOSEPH MOURET
- Rondeau 16

WOLFGANG AMADEUS MOZART
- Sonata 16

MODESTE MUSSORGSKY
- Great Gate of Kiev 3
- Pictures at an Exhibition 24

JOHANN STRAUSS JR.
- Adele's Song 7

PETER I. TCHAIKOVSKY
- Waltz in Five (from *Symphony No. 6*) 30

World Music

AFRICAN
- Jibuli 20
- Sukuru Ito 24

AMERICAN
- Children's Shoes 3
- I Walk the Road Again 17
- The Keel Row 7
- Keepin' Secrets 7
- Sit Down, Sister 19
- Star Spangled Banner 15
- Turkey in the Straw 12

AUSTRALIAN
- Australian Folk Song 5

ENGLISH
- Greensleeves 17
- Molly Bann 4
- Wolsey's Wilde 27

FRENCH
- Pat-A-Pan 5
- French National Anthem 27

IRISH
- The Pretty Girl 13

JAPANESE
- Song of the Shakuhachi 28

LATIN AMERICAN
- Cielito Lindo 30

MALAYSIAN
- Suriram's Song 20

NATIVE AMERICAN INDIAN
- Song of the Weeping Spirit 9

RUSSIAN
- The Sledgehammer Song 5

SCOTTISH
- Scottish Legend 9
- The Young Chevalier 30